I0479786

The Youngest Leadership

—————————————————————

How to Build Leadership
Qualities in Teens

Copyright © 2023 by Amelia S.B - All rights reserved.

No portion of this book may be reproduced in any form without written permission from the publisher or author, except as permitted by U.S. copyright law.

This publication is designed to provide accurate and authoritative information in regard to the subject matter covered. It is sold with the understanding that neither the author nor the publisher is engaged in rendering legal, investment, accounting or other professional services. While the publisher and author have used their best efforts in preparing this book, they make no representations or warranties with respect to the accuracy or completeness of the contents of this book and specifically disclaim any implied warranties of merchantability or fitness for a particular purpose. This book also contains affiliate links, which means that if you use one of the product links, we'll receive a small commission. This helps support the project and allows us to continue to make books and other content like this. Thank you for your support.

No warranty may be created or extended by sales representatives or written sales materials. The advice and strategies contained herein may not be suitable for your situation. You should consult with a professional when appropriate. Neither the publisher nor the author shall be liable for any loss of profit or any other commercial damages, including but not limited to special, incidental, consequential, personal, or other damages.

Publishing Assistant by Digimasterz.net

Table of Contents

Introduction

Leadership abilities are crucial for both professional and personal development. Everybody who wants to succeed in life has to possess this skill set. Yet, leadership abilities are not only for adults; teens also need them for success in life. A young person's life may be greatly impacted by their capacity to lead and influence others, which can shape their destiny in various ways.

A thorough handbook titled "The Youngest Leadership: How to Develop Leadership Qualities in Teenagers" intends to assist youngsters in honing their leadership abilities. Readers of this book will acquire the skills and information necessary to excel as leaders in their personal and professional lives.

The book's first chapter defines leadership and its many guises, including transactional, transformational, and servant leadership. It looks at traits like vision, integrity, empathy, confidence, and resilience, as well as those that make a good leader. The chapter concludes by outlining the advantages of adolescent leadership development, including better academic achievement, enhanced communication abilities, more self-esteem, and more prospects for success.

The second chapter is dedicated to personal growth and self-awareness. It addresses issues including knowing oneself, assets, and liabilities, fostering self-assurance and a good self-perception, gaining skills for handling stress and emotions, and using mindfulness methods.

The third chapter explores interpersonal and communication skills. It offers advice on improving communication abilities such as active listening, reading body language, and verbal and nonverbal communication. The chapter also stresses the value of forming connections, cooperating with others, and growing empathy and conflict-resolution abilities.

The fourth chapter covers time management and goal-setting. It explains the value of using

SMART goals and action planning techniques to create attainable goals and action plans. The chapter also offers readers advice on how to prioritize tasks, use time management techniques, stop putting things off, and deal with distractions.

The topic of decision-making and problem-solving is covered in the fifth chapter. It addresses issues like making informed decisions, weighing the pros and cons, recognising issues and determining their root causes, and coming up with original solutions and acting on them.

The sixth chapter examines various leadership philosophies and techniques. It teaches youngsters when to employ various leadership philosophies, including autocratic, democratic, and laissez-faire leadership. The chapter also emphasizes the significance of empowerment and delegation, creating a leadership vision, and leading with purpose.

The seventh chapter focuses on cooperation and teamwork. It advises teenagers on creating productive teams, encouraging cooperation, comprehending group dynamics, establishing trust and respect, and settling disputes.

The eighth chapter explores morality and civic duty. It highlights the significance of moral decision-making and moral leadership. The chapter also emphasizes how important it is to cultivate empathy and social responsibility, make moral choices, and accept responsibility for one's conduct.

The ninth chapter offers teens helpful advice on applying leadership abilities to the real world. It addresses issues like locating leadership opportunities in school, extracurricular activities, and community service; getting ready for college and future careers; emphasizing leadership skills on resumes and applications; building a personal brand and professional network; and enhancing leadership skills throughout one's life. In short, this book is a vital resource for teens who wish to grow as leaders. Let's dive deep into it.

Chapter 1: Understanding Leadership

A person's personal and professional life may be significantly impacted by their leadership abilities, an essential talent. It enables people to lead, inspire, and encourage others toward a shared objective. We will examine the value of developing leadership qualities in teens in this chapter as well as the many leadership philosophies.

1.1 Leadership and its Types

Leadership is the capacity to persuade, uplift, and direct others toward a shared objective. It is the skill of inspiring others to strive towards a common goal. Leadership may be shown at whatever level of a company, from the front lines to the executive suite.

Depending on their particular traits, ideals, and the company's demands, people might embrace a variety of leadership philosophies. Among the most popular leadership philosophies are the following:

Transactional Leadership

Leadership in the transactional model is focused on getting things done, working within the organization's current framework, and evaluating success using the established incentives and punishments.

Formal authority and positions of duty are hallmarks of transactional leadership. Performance evaluations are the most popular tool for evaluating an employee's contributions in organizations with a transactional or managerial leadership structure.

The following are the duties of transactional leaders:

- Establish objectives, and provide detailed instructions on how the employee should proceed and what they may expect in return for their hard work.
- Help others improve by giving them constructive criticism.
- Put more effort into streamlining regular processes and demonstrating respect for the status quo rather than introducing novel ideas.

- Put in place and standardize procedures to increase output and efficiency.
- React to results that differ from expectations and determine what needs to be done to get back on track.

Leadership in the Transactional Model

Leaders who choose this mode are more concerned with keeping things running smoothly. Leaders that operate in a transactional mode rely on benefits, threats and various incentives to inspire their teams to give their all.

Transactional leaders encourage their teams by offering material benefits in exchange for hard work. Such a leader is only concerned with the company's day-to-day operations rather than with the long-term goals of expanding the company's market share.

It is built on communicating expectations to subordinates and motivating them to act on them via positive and negative reinforcement. Transactional leaders define the expectations of their followers' roles and direct them towards achieving those objectives. Interactions between leaders and subordinates are the primary emphasis of transactional leadership, often known as managerial leadership.

At the heart of transactional leadership is that a leader who exercises authority and command over subordinates or followers should incentivise those individuals to carry out the leader's wishes. Despite its drawbacks, it may be useful in some scenarios. A transactional approach may be useful when issues are straightforward and easy to solve.

In complicated circumstances, when input from group members is necessary, there are better approaches than transactional leadership since it does not inspire group members to explore for answers to issues or to participate creatively.

Transactional Leadership Traits

- Very left-brained
- Often exhibit rigidity.
- Unwilling to adapt.
- Considering just the immediate future.
- Prefer well-defined processes and guidelines.
- Thriving in situations where strict conformity to norms is required.

Pros of transactional leadership

- The followers of a transactional leader are rewarded because it is in their best interest.
- It provides a clear framework for indefinitely repeatable settings, complex systems with repeated operations, and massive enterprises.

- Very proficient at accomplishing immediate objectives.
- Employees decide disciplinary measures and financial incentives.

Consequences of a Transactional Leadership Style

- Monetary or other material incentives are the only kind of reward that the employee will accept.
- With predetermined outcomes in mind, originality is stifled.
- There needs to be a recognition system for the efforts.

Leadership styles that are examples of transactional leadership

In times of crisis or when following a strict protocol is essential to completing the task, the transactional leadership style is likely to prevail.

- Hewlett-Packard, for example, is a large firm well-known for its effective use of management by exception, and this approach may also be helpful for them.

- Many top-level military officers, CEOs of multinational corporations, and NFL head coaches are examples of transactional leaders.
- Police departments and other emergency response teams may benefit greatly from transactional leadership.

Excellent illustration of a transactional leader is Bill Gates

In 1955, William Gates entered the world in Seattle. When he was a teenager, he and Paul Allen met at Lakeside School, where they had a passion for creating computer programmes.

After Gates enrolled at Harvard University, Allen relocated to Boston to work as a computer programmer for Honeywell. Microsoft was founded in 1975, and by the time Gates was 23 years old in 1978, the business had already earned $2.5 million. Microsoft released Windows to the public in 1985.

Bill Gates ranks high among the world's wealthiest and most powerful individuals. To ensure everything is on the right track, he would personally visit teams and ask probing questions. He gave consistent incentives to keep them motivating and grow his company.

Transformational Leadership

Transformational leadership emphasizes inspiring and encouraging team members to work towards a common goal. This kind of leadership, founded on "leading by example," is often used in companies where internal benefits like personal development or a feeling of purpose drive workers.

Transformational leaders motivate and inspire by articulating a compelling vision and giving their team members a feeling of purpose. They encourage risk-taking, innovation, and originality in the workplace and allow team members to own their work. Transformational leaders foster strong ties and community among their team members.

Servant Leadership

A leadership approach called servant leadership puts the needs of others first. This leadership approach, centering on "putting others first," is often used in businesses with a social goal, such as nonprofits and the medical field.

The requirements of their team members come before their own servant leader. To support and assist their team members in achieving their objectives, they work to understand their needs and ambitions. Servant leaders inspire team members to collaborate and be inclusive to achieve a shared objective.

Real life scenario

We'll use the example of a high school sports team to demonstrate the various leadership philosophies.

A transactional leader could establish clear goals for the squad and provide incentives for good work, much more playing time, or a slot in the starting lineup. They could keep a close eye on things and provide the team members feedback depending on their successes.

A compelling team vision, such as winning the championship or fostering an inclusive and team-oriented culture, may motivate the team members and inspire transformative leadership. They could provide the team members the tools they need to take ownership of their job, such as including them in decision-making or giving them chances for skill- and personal development.

A servant leader could put the needs of the team members ahead of their own, for example, by offering assistance and resources to enable them to meet objectives or overcome obstacles. They could encourage team members to support one another and strive towards a shared objective, such as building a collaborative and inclusive atmosphere.

In conclusion, being aware of the many leadership styles may help people refine their leadership abilities and improve their effectiveness in both their personal and professional life.

1.2 Exploring the traits and qualities of effective leaders

Effective leaders have various leadership qualities that they execute in real life.

Vision

Vision is one of the most crucial qualities of successful leaders. Vision is the capacity to see a future distinct from the present and to motivate others to strive towards it. In this section, we will discuss what vision is in the context of leadership, why it is important, and how to cultivate it.

Vision in Leadership

A leader's ability to generate and communicate a compelling vision of the 'ideal future state' to his/her followers is known as a vision in leadership. It entails having a clear vision for where you want to go and what you want to accomplish and the capacity to inspire and encourage people to work towards that goal.

Why It Matters

For many reasons, having a distinct and engaging vision is crucial. First, it gives the organization or group being led, a purpose and direction. People may feel lost or unsure of what they are working towards without a clear vision, resulting in disengagement and a lack of motivation.

Second, having a clear vision may encourage people to believe in you and give you credit. People are more inclined to believe and follow a leader when they clearly understand where they are heading and how they intend to get there.

Last but not least, a compelling vision may assist in drawing in and keeping skilled and motivated followers. Humans want a feeling of belonging to something greater than themselves, and a compelling vision may provide them both.

Vision Formation for Leaders

These are some tactics:

- **Consider your values and objectives.**

It's crucial to have a clear knowledge of your beliefs and objectives before creating a vision. Spend some time considering your top priorities, your goals, and the sort of effect you want to have on the world.

- **SWOT analysis should be done**

You may find the internal and external aspects that can influence your business or group through a SWOT analysis (Strengths, Weaknesses, Opportunities, and Threats). You may then utilize this knowledge to shape your vision.

- **Team together with others.**

Everyone in the company or group should have a clear vision. Work with others to reach a consensus on the ideal vision and the best ways to realize it.

- **Effective communication**

It's crucial to properly convey your vision to your followers when you've formed it. Employ language that is clear and persuasive, and make sure to highlight the advantages of working towards the goal.

Example of Leaders having a vision

In the past, there have been many outstanding leaders who had distinct and appealing visions. Here are a few illustrations:

King, Martin Luther Jr. King's dream of a society where everyone is treated fairly, decently, and respectfully inspired a generation. He resulted in important improvements to the legislation governing civil rights.

Elon Musk: Musk has motivated many individuals to strive towards these objectives with his vision of an electric vehicle, renewable energy, and space exploration-filled future.

Mahatma Gandhi – Gandhi inspired a country and ended British rule with his vision of a free and independent India.

To sum up, having a distinct and appealing vision is a crucial quality of successful leaders. It gives the organization or group direction, and a purpose helps to establish credibility and trust among followers and may draw in and keep skilled and motivated followers. It's crucial to consider your beliefs and objectives, do a SWOT analysis, work with others, and communicate clearly to build a vision as a leader. Elon Musk, Mahatma Gandhi, and Martin Luther King Jr. are a few examples of visionary leaders.

Integrity

One of the most crucial qualities of successful leaders is integrity. It is a fundamental trait that supports leaders in fostering loyalty, establishing the tone for their group or team, and fostering trust. This section will examine what integrity is, why it's important, and how emerging leaders can develop it.

Describe integrity

It is being sincere, moral, and constant in one's activities, principles, approaches, standards, and results. It entails acting honestly and openly in interactions with others, keeping one's word and commitments, and standing up for what is right, even when it is challenging or controversial.

Why Is Integrity Important?

For several reasons, integrity is necessary for effective leadership. It first aids in fostering trust among leaders and their followers. People are more likely to accept a leader's judgment and adhere to their instructions if they believe that person to be honest and moral. This is crucial because people need to trust that their leaders have their best interests in mind when facing a crisis or unclear situation.

Second, fostering an environment of responsibility requires integrity. Leaders who uphold high moral standards for themselves create a good example for their group or company. This promotes a culture where everyone is expected to honor themselves and take responsibility for their actions.

Finally, integrity is necessary to develop a reputation as a dependable, effective, and trustworthy leader. Integrity-driven leaders are more likely to enjoy their peers' respect, their followers' trust, and success in their pursuits.

How Can Future Leaders Develop Integrity?

Integrity development is a lifelong process that calls for self-examination, self-awareness, and a dedication to upholding moral principles.

Here are some techniques young leaders can employ to foster integrity:

- *Establish high ethical standards for yourself.*

Setting high ethical standards and holding yourself responsible is essential for leaders. This entails acting with integrity, openness, and consistency in line with your beliefs, ideals, and values.

- *Transparency and open communication*

Leaders should practice transparency and open communication because they inspire trust in their followers. This entails being upfront with facts, honest about your intentions, and accepting responsibility for your errors.

- *Maintain your commitments and promises*

Establishing trust with your followers requires that you keep your commitments and promises. This entails acting in a trustworthy, dependable, and consistent manner.

- *Get feedback and take criticism to heart*

Integrity-building requires being receptive to criticism. This entails being prepared to hear all viewpoints, learn from your errors, and adjust as necessary.

- *Act with courage and conviction*

Sometimes, it takes courage and conviction to do the right thing. This entails standing up for your principles even when challenging or unpopular. Leaders that take courageous and steadfast action motivate followers to follow suit.

Examples of Integrity in Leadership

There are numerous examples of leaders who have displayed integrity in their deeds and manner of leadership. Many instances include:

Mahatma Gandhi: Gandhi is regarded as one of the 20th century's most important leaders. He is renowned for his passion for nonviolent resistance and unyielding adherence to his beliefs.

Nelson Mandela is another prominent figure whose integrity is highly recognized. His dedication to abolishing apartheid in South Africa and his steadfast commitment to justice and equality have made him well renowned.

Ruth Bader Ginsburg: Ginsburg paved the way for women's rights in the legal profession. She is renowned for her passion for justice, unshakable adherence to her values, and readiness to defend what she believes in.

Empathy

Empathy is the capacity to comprehend and experience another's emotions. It entails understanding the feelings of others, placing oneself in their situation, and responding properly. Although empathy is frequently referred to as a "soft skill," it is crucial for successful leadership. Empathetic leaders are better equipped to interact with others, form bonds with them, and make choices that will help their teams.

The value of compassion in leadership

Because it enables leaders to connect with people, foster trust and respect, and elicit devotion and commitment from followers, empathy is an important quality for effective leadership. Empathetic leaders pay attention to the worries of their team members, identify their assets and limitations, and provide the care and support they require. Leaders may foster a supportive workplace with empathy where employees feel valued and inspired to perform at their highest level.

Techniques for Fostering Empathy

It is possible to improve empathy through repetition and self-analysis. The following techniques can aid teenagers in growing their capacity for empathy.

Active listening

This entails paying attention to what others are saying without interruption, judgment, or distraction, which is one of the essential elements of empathy. Teenagers should concentrate on being present in conversations, asking questions, and confirming their understanding to build active listening abilities.

Placing Yourself in Others' Shoes

Empathy requires being aware of the thoughts and feelings of others. Teens can master this talent by placing themselves in other people's shoes, reflecting on their feelings, and responding appropriately. They can learn empathy and understanding of others using this method.

Right Language

Using language that indicates understanding and compassion, such as "I hear you," "I understand how you feel," or "That must be tough for you," is a practice in empathic communication. Teens can practice using human language in everyday interactions with friends, family, and peers.

Various Cultures and Perspectives

Adolescents can learn empathy by being exposed to many cultures, viewpoints, and lifestyles. These are examples of reading books, viewing films or documentaries, or visiting various locations. Teenagers can learn to accept and comprehend others' differences as well as build empathy through being exposed to a variety of situations.

Oprah Winfrey & Nelson Mandela Example

Oprah Winfrey is a notable example of an empathetic leader. She tried to bring about positive change in her community and showed a profound knowledge of people's needs and feelings.

Oprah Winfrey is renowned for her empathic communication approach, which includes active listening, sharing personal stories, and considering the perspectives of others. Through her talk show, she has forged connections with millions of viewers, given voice to underrepresented groups, and motivated viewers to make positive changes.

Nelson Mandela is an illustration of an empathic leader who utilized his comprehension of other people's views to effect constructive change. He toiled diligently as South Africa's first black president to end apartheid, advance peace, and unite his nation. He exhibited empathy by listening to both sides, accepting the anguish and pain of others, and seeking out a middle ground.

Self-Esteem

High self-esteem is a crucial quality in successful leaders. Self-esteem is a positive assessment of one's worth. Those who have high standards for themselves:

- Feel welcomed and appreciated for who they are
- exhibit confidence in their abilities
- take pride in their accomplishments.

Those that lack confidence:

- be humiliated by their self
- are critical of themselves and feel they are bad

The origins of one's sense of self-worth

Individuals such as parents, educators, and others around us have the power to shape our sense of self-worth. They boost our confidence when they highlight our best qualities. We grow in self-acceptance when others are patient with us when we make errors. Likeness comes when we have friends and can socialize with them. Yet it's tough to feel good about yourself if grownups reprimand you more often than compliment you.

Low self-esteem may also result from bullying or cruel mocking from family members or classmates. Negative comments may leave lasting scars on a person's psyche. Fortunately, things aren't doomed to remain hopeless forever. Your inner monologue heavily influences your self-perception. Thinking down on yourself like "I'm such a loser" or "I'll never make friends" is unhealthy.

Several perspectives exist on the same issues. The harsh remarks of others are sometimes the source of that inner voice. Or the tough moments we've had to endure. Our inner critic may be nothing more than our self-criticism. But we have the power to alter that internal dialogue. Our positive self-image is something we can cultivate.

Gaining the ability to do tasks

Learning anything new, whether reading, adding, drawing, or constructing, makes us happy. Just do something active like playing a sport, making music, writing an essay, or riding a bike. Prepare the meal and clean the vehicle. Assist a neighbor, walk a dog. Learning and doing new things may boost your confidence. Take a breath and survey your accomplishments. Soak in the joy that it brings you.

Nonetheless, we might be excessively critical of ourselves at times. None of us believes that our efforts are sufficient. Negative thoughts like "It's not perfect" or "I can't do it well enough" prevent us from gaining confidence.

Steps to boost Self Esteem

There are steps to boost your self-esteem. A late start is better than no start at all. Some suggestions to help you feel better about yourself:

Maintain positive relationships with those in your life

Some individuals constantly bring you down with their actions. The words and actions of others uplift you. Master the art of positive relationships. Get along with people who make you feel good about who you are. Select a group of friends who accept you for who you are. Become that kind of friend to others around you.

Inspire yourself by doing positive self-talk

Pay attention to the thoughts floating about in your brain. Can it be looked at as overly harsh? Do you criticize yourself too much? Try keeping a journal of your self-talk for a few days. Flip through the items on your list. Would you say these things to a close friend? Instead, reward them such that they are honest, reasonable, and considerate. Take the time to read your new phrases often. Put in the time and effort until that thinking style becomes second nature.

Don't try to fix the imperfect

Maintaining a high standard of excellence is always recommended. Yet, if you believe you must be flawless, you will never be satisfied with anything less. The best you can do is to be acceptable. Have some pride in it. Get assistance if you can't move over your demand for perfection independently.

Make plans and do your best to achieve them

Take care of yourself, and you'll feel better about yourself. You may aim to improve your nutrition, fitness, or academic performance. Have your sights set on something. The next step is to formulate a strategy for carrying it out. Do what you set out to do. Monitor your development. Take pride in your accomplishments.

In your mind, "I've been consistent about working out for 45 minutes daily. Generally,

I'm pleased with the results. That pace is sustainable for me."

Pay attention to the positive

Have you been so used to discussing difficulties that you can only perceive them? It's simple to dwell on the negative. But you'll only feel worse if you don't counteract the negative with some positive thoughts. Try to stop yourself the next time you start a pity party about yourself or your day. Consider a positive alternative.

Donate, and aid those in need

Giving to others may be a powerful catalyst for inner growth. Walk for a good cause, tutor a student, or help clean up your community. Assist with household or academic tasks. Adopt a consistent approach of fairness and kindness. Do actions that highlight the admirable qualities you possess. No matter how tiny, the satisfaction you get from making a difference may do wonders for your sense of personal worth.

Confidence

For a leader to be effective, confidence is a critical quality. Confident leaders encourage followers to believe in their potential and the team or organization's goals and objectives. The significance of confidence as a leadership quality and methods for fostering and sustaining it will be discussed in this section.

Knowing how to be confident

Being confident is having faith in oneself and one's skills to make choices and act. Arrogance or excessive confidence, which can impair judgment and erode trust in others, is not the same as confidence.

The value of leadership confidence

Leadership requires confidence because it enables leaders to:

- Confident executives inspire and motivate their teams to believe in their potential and the goals and objectives of the company.

- Taking Action: Self-assured leaders act and choose without second-guessing. They don't doubt themselves or put things off, which can result in lost opportunities.
- Embrace Change: Flexible and adaptable leaders can accept change. They don't hesitate to take chances or try new things.
- Difficulties can be overcome with elegance and resiliency by leaders who are confident in their abilities. Instead of letting failure demoralize them, they learn from their errors and seize the chance to advance.

Gaining Self-Assurance as a Leader

Instead of being a natural quality, confidence can be acquired via deliberate practice and effort. Here are some methods for boosting your leadership confidence and keeping it there:

Establish Goals: Achieving your goals is a terrific approach to boosting your confidence.

Larger goals should be broken down into more manageable tasks, and you should recognize your progress as you go.

Gain Expertise: Increasing your knowledge in a certain field will make you feel more confident. Look for chances to learn and develop, such as attending conferences or taking courses.

Individuals Who Believe in You and Support Your Goals Should Be Around You: Surround yourself with people who support you and your ambitions. Look for friends and mentors who can provide direction and encouragement.

Practice Self-Care: Confidence is maintained through taking care of oneself. Get enough rest, work out frequently, and maintain a balanced diet.

Practice visualization: By seeing oneself succeeding in difficult circumstances, visualization techniques can allow one to develop confidence. Imagine yourself guiding your team with the assurance of success.

Practice being assertive: Confidence is greatly influenced by assertiveness. Practice asserting yourself with dignity and assurance, and develop the ability to say "no" when necessary.

Leaders with confidence

Many effective leaders have made confidence a central aspect of their leadership style. Oprah Winfrey, for instance, is renowned for her self-assurance and capacity to uplift and motivate people. "I believe that one of life's greatest risks is never daring to risk," she once said.

Another illustration is Steve Jobs, who was renowned for his certainty in his vision for Apple and his capacity to motivate his staff to produce ground-breaking goods.

In short, for a leader to be effective, confidence is a critical quality. Confidence in oneself and one's talents enables leaders to move forward, adapt to change, and overcome obstacles. Building and sustaining confidence takes deliberate work and practice. It is a skill that can be acquired and improved through time. Leaders can grow and sustain their confidence in themselves and their skills by creating goals, acquiring expertise, surrounding themselves with encouraging individuals, engaging in self-care, visualizing success, and being aggressive.

Resilience

A crucial quality for effective leaders is resilience. It allows them to persevere despite difficulties and setbacks while moving closer to their objectives. Strong purpose, steadfast drive, and the capacity to recover from setbacks are characteristics of resilient leaders.

Recognizing Resilience

Resilience is the capacity to overcome challenges, setbacks, and adversity. It involves handling pressure and stress, adjusting to change, and returning from setbacks. Resilient leaders can keep their motivation and focus intact even when things don't go according to plan.

Resilient leaders understand that failure is a necessary component of learning and take advantage of it as a chance to advance. They can remain composed under duress and upbeat in the face of difficulties and preserve their sense of humor even under trying circumstances.

Characteristics of Resilient Leaders

Resilient leaders have some important characteristics, including:

- Resilient leaders keep a positive attitude in the face of difficulties. They can identify possibilities in difficulties and concentrate on things they have control over rather than those they do not.

- Determined and persistent leaders are resilient. Despite setbacks and challenges, they are prepared to invest the time and effort necessary to accomplish their objectives.
- Flexibility and adaptability are characteristics of resilient leaders. They can change their plans and approaches as necessary to address unforeseen situations.
- Resilient leaders have high levels of emotional intelligence, allowing them to control their emotions effectively. They can keep composure under duress and have an optimistic outlook in facing difficulties.
- Resilient leaders have faith in their abilities and identities. Even in the face of uncertainty, they can take calculated risks and render difficult decisions.
- Strong leaders have a growth mentality and see failure as a chance for personal and professional improvement. They are constantly looking for methods to grow and become better.

Leadership Instances of Resilience

There are numerous instances of resilient leaders in the past and the present. Abraham Lincoln is one such example. Despite his life's many setbacks and disappointments, Lincoln maintained his determination and persisted in the face of difficulty. He persevered in his endeavors and finally became one of the most admired presidents in American history, despite suffering numerous electoral defeats and personal sorrow.

Harry Potter author J.K. Rowling is another illustration of a resilient leader. Before her books finally became successful, Rowling received countless publisher rejections. The hardships she endured included a divorce and her mother's death, yet she persisted in her determination to succeed.

In short, for a leader to be successful, resilience is a crucial quality. It allows individuals to overcome obstacles and setbacks, stay motivated and focused, and accomplish their objectives. Optimism, persistence, adaptability, emotional intelligence, confidence, and a growth mindset are characteristics of resilient leaders. Young leaders can become more resilient and better prepared to handle challenges by cultivating these skills and qualities.

1.3 Leadership's Value in Academic Environments

On both an individual and group level, effective leadership has a substantial impact on academic performance. This section will examine how fostering a leadership culture can enhance academic performance and foster a supportive learning environment.

Leadership abilities are crucial in academic environments, where teens must cooperate, communicate, and work towards shared objectives. Leaders can create a favorable learning environment with the right talents, which can significantly affect academic success. Successful leaders can encourage and inspire their followers to put forth extra effort, maintain concentration, and accomplish their objectives.

Setting goals

For academic achievement, setting goals is essential. Good leaders may assist people in setting realistic goals and developing plans of action to reach them. Individuals can maintain focus, order their priorities, and monitor their progress by setting goals.

Management of time

Successful leaders are aware of how crucial time management is for academic success. People can learn from leaders how to organize their time effectively, set priorities for their work, and make a timetable. Those with good time management abilities can keep up with their academics, resist procrastination, and fulfill deadlines.

Clear Communication

In academic environments, clear communication is vital. Strong communicators can aid others in developing their active listening, verbal and nonverbal communication, and collaboration abilities. Those with better communication skills can participate more actively in class discussions, comprehend the course material, and collaborate well with their peers.

Fixing issues

Good leaders may assist people in acquiring problem-solving abilities, which are crucial in academic environments. People can learn from leaders how to examine issues, find their sources, and develop workable solutions. Individuals can overcome academic obstacles, achieve in their studies, and flourish in their future employment by acquiring problem-solving skills.

Motivation

Strong motivators can encourage followers to put in extra effort, maintain attention, and succeed in their academic objectives. Leaders can foster a supportive learning atmosphere, offer helpful criticism, and acknowledge the accomplishments of others. By offering inspiration, people can find a purpose, remain dedicated to their studies, and succeed academically.

Mentoring Initiatives

Mentoring programs can enhance academic achievement. Strong leaders can mentor their mentees and offer them support, encouragement, and motivation. Mentors can support their mentees in developing study habits, academic goal-setting, and academic focus

Programs for Student Leadership

Student leadership programs can assist people in growing as leaders and enhancing their academic success. These programs allow participants to assume leadership roles, work with their colleagues, and hone their problem-solving abilities.

Group Assignments

Group projects can be useful for fostering leadership qualities and raising academic achievement. Good group leaders may mentor their members, guarantee that everyone contributes to the project, and facilitate conflict resolution. When people collaborate, they can learn from one another, develop their communication skills, and produce better results than they could have done alone.

Having strong leadership abilities can have a big impact on academic success. People can achieve in their education, find a purpose, and flourish in their future employment by developing leadership qualities such as goal planning, time management, communication, problem-solving, and motivation. Good leaders can inspire and motivate their peers, foster a positive learning atmosphere, and support people in achieving their academic objectives.

1.4 Improved communication skills

An effective leader must have the ability to communicate effectively. A leader may develop trust, motivate people, communicate effectively, and foster a healthy work atmosphere. This section will examine how young leaders can develop their leadership skills and become more effective communicators.

Good communication abilities are essential for a leader since they foster rapport and generate trust among team members. Leaders who can express themselves properly can effectively share their thoughts and vision with their team. Good communication abilities are also helpful in settling disputes and encouraging group cooperation.

Building Verbal Communication Skills: The capacity to communicate effectively through speech is called verbal communication skills. It covers things like word choice, pronunciation, and vocal inflection. A successful leader must be able to express their ideas and views clearly and concisely. Good verbal communication abilities aid leaders in getting their point through, inspiring their teams, and developing trust.

Improving Nonverbal Communication Skills: The ability to communicate through body language, facial expressions, and tone of voice is called nonverbal communication. Effective nonverbal cue reading and interpretation skills are essential for a leader. This facilitates establishing a rapport with team members and demonstrating empathy for their issues.

Active Listening: Successful communication involves listening as well as speaking. A leader needs to be able to listen actively. It entails listening carefully, posing questions, and clearing up any confusion. A leader who actively listens to their team members can better understand their needs, viewpoints, and needs, which fosters a productive workplace.

Nonverbal Communication: Body language, facial gestures, and voice tone are all part of it. Nonverbal communication is an effective way for a leader to connect with their team since it can say more than words. Leaders can create a positive work atmosphere with strong nonverbal communication abilities.

Developing Relationships and Cooperating with Others: An effective leader must collaborate and build strong bonds with others. This entails fostering empathy for fellow team members, working well, and resolving problems. Building relationships and cooperating with others require effective communication skills.

Building Empathy: The capacity to comprehend and share the feelings of others is known as empathy. A successful leader must be able to relate to the issues and worries of their team. Active listening and paying attention to nonverbal signs are necessary for developing empathy. Empathy promotes a healthy work atmosphere and aids in the development of trust.

Collaboration abilities are the ability to cooperate successfully to achieve a common objective. To accomplish organizational goals, a successful leader must be able to work collaboratively with team members. Collaboration requires effective communication because it is how ideas are communicated, relationships are formed, and trust is established.

Settlement of Conflict: Any workplace will inevitably have conflict. A successful leader must be able to manage disagreements. This entails determining the conflict's underlying cause, paying attention to both sides, and coming to an amicable agreement. To develop a positive workplace culture and show empathy for the concerns of team members, effective communication skills are crucial for conflict resolution.

In conclusion, youngsters who want to become leaders must have strong communication abilities. Effective communication requires various abilities, including active listening, relationship-building, verbal and nonverbal communication development, and conflict resolution. A successful leader must work well with others and cultivate empathy for their team members. Good communication abilities foster teamwork, foster the development of trust, and foster a positive work atmosphere.

1.5 Building Higher self-esteem

We have discussed it earlier as well. Here we will be more specific on tips to achieve greater self-esteem. Self-esteem is crucial because it enables leaders to make self-assured decisions, inspire others, and encourage their teams. Leaders with a stronger sense of self-worth are more likely to have confidence in their skills and a positive view of life. Furthermore, because they have a strong feeling of their value, leaders with greater levels of self-esteem are less likely to be affected by criticism, failure, or setbacks.

Advantages of Greater Self-Esteem for Leaders: Leaders that have higher self-esteem frequently reap some advantages, such as:

Confidence and Assertiveness: Leaders with a stronger sense of self-worth are more aggressive in their leadership, communication, and decision-making.

Resilience: Those with higher self-esteem can endure difficulties and challenges, recover from failure, and overcome adversities.

Positive Outlook: Leaders that have better self-esteem are more upbeat and pessimistic, which increases motivation, vigor, and involvement.

Creativity: Those who have higher self-esteem tend to be more innovative, risk-taking, and creative, which can result in more success and progress.

How to Achieve and Sustain Greater Self-Esteem in Leaders

Self-reflection: By considering their past accomplishments, strengths, and successes, leaders can raise their self-worth. Due to this process, they develop a sense of pride, self-worth, and confidence.

Positive Self-Talk: Leaders can retain stronger self-esteem by employing positive self-talk, which entails supporting and validating oneself. Through it, leaders develop resilience, stay motivated, and overcome negative thoughts and feelings.

Accept Challenges: Leaders can increase their self-esteem by accepting challenges and taking measured risks. They gain confidence, learn from their mistakes, and overcome challenges thanks to this process.

Ask for Feedback: Leaders who ask for feedback from their team and coworkers tend to have higher self-esteem. Thanks to this feedback, they get insight into their strengths and limitations, develop their leadership abilities, and establish credibility with their team.

Leaders with higher self-esteem include

Oprah Winfrey: Oprah Winfrey is a well-known talk show host, philanthropist, and media executive. She credits her strong self-esteem, which she built through encouraging self-talk and self-affirmations, for her success.

Richard Branson: The Virgin Group's founder is renowned for his innovative and daring approach to leadership. He has grown to have a high sense of self through accepting challenges, receiving criticism, and overcoming failures.

Indra Nooyi: She is an accomplished businesswoman and executive who served as the former CEO of PepsiCo. She established a strong sense of self-worth by embracing her cultural identity, receiving criticism, and concentrating on her skills.

Higher self-esteem is necessary for effective leadership in light of the preceding. Higher self-esteem in leaders is associated with greater success and development because these individuals are more resilient, creative, and positive. Leaders can increase and maintain their sense of worth by reflecting on their actions, talking to themselves positively, accepting challenges, and asking for feedback.

1.6 Greater opportunities for success

Success in every sector depends on being able to lead effectively. Successful leaders are distinguished from others by characteristics that help them forge a vision, motivate their group, and accomplish their objectives. The enhanced chances for success are among the most important advantages of having good leaders. This section will examine how good leadership traits and skills increase the likelihood of success.

Clear Goals

Establishing clear goals and having a clear picture of their desired outcomes is a quality of effective leaders. They initiate specific objectives and effectively convey them to their staff. Leaders may motivate their team to work towards the same objective by having a clear vision, which ultimately results in higher success. For instance, Apple co-founder Steve Jobs had a distinct vision for developing goods that were not only cutting-edge but also user-friendly. This vision inspired the development of legendary products like the iPod, iPhone, and iPad, which revolutionized the IT sector and elevated Apple to the status of one of the most prosperous businesses in the entire world.

Strong Decisions

Effective leaders possess strong decision-making abilities. They can examine options, analyze information, and reach well-informed conclusions that benefit the group and the company. These choices are frequently made using knowledge, wisdom, and intuition. Leaders can direct their teams toward success by making wise judgments. For instance, General Motors CEO Mary Barra made the difficult choice to recall millions of vehicles to address safety concerns, ultimately saving lives and restoring the company's reputation.

Enhanced Communication

Good communicators make for effective leaders. They can communicate their team's expectations, vision, and goals. They are also adept at giving constructive criticism and active listening, contributing to a collaborative and open culture. Effective communication requires building great relationships with team members, stakeholders, and customers. Tony Hsieh, the previous CEO of Zappos, established a culture of openness and transparency, which aided in developing a devoted customer base and a highly motivated team.

Remain Resilient

Successful leaders can adjust and remain resilient despite difficulties and setbacks. They may shift course rapidly as things change, and do not give up lightly. Leaders can handle ambiguous situations and discover fresh possibilities for success by being flexible and resilient. For instance, Jeff Bezos, the CEO of Amazon, was able to adjust to the shifting market trends and turn Amazon from an online bookshop into a global e-commerce behemoth that provides a variety of goods and services.

Self-assurance

Strong leaders have self-assurance in both themselves and their teams. With this confidence, their squad is motivated to take chances and go beyond their comfort zones. Also, it fosters a culture of experimentation and creativity, which increases success. Elon Musk, the CEO of Tesla and SpaceX, has a lot of faith in his team's capacity to create ground-breaking goods like electric automobiles and reusable rockets. The success of both businesses has been fueled in part by this assurance.

In summary, effective leaders have special skills and characteristics that increase their chances of success. Leaders can motivate their teams, overcome obstacles, and uncover new prospects for success by having a clear vision, strong decision-making and communication skills, adaptability and resilience, and confidence. To be more effective, aspiring leaders can learn from the examples of successful leaders and develop similar traits and qualities inside themselves.

Chapter 2: Self-Awareness and Personal Development

2.1 Understanding oneself

A variety of abilities and traits are included in leadership, which has several facets. Self-reflection is one of these necessary qualities for good leadership. In this chapter, we will examine the significance of self-reflection as an important quality for successful leaders and how it may aid people in realizing their leadership potential.

What does introspection entail?

Examining one's feelings, ideas, and actions to understand better oneself is the process of self-reflection. It entails being truthful with oneself, accepting positive and negative traits, and being receptive to criticism. Self-reflection is essential to human development because it helps people learn from their experiences and make wiser choices in the future.

Self-reflection is important in leadership because effective leadership needs a thorough awareness of oneself, others, and the environment in which one works. Self-reflection aids in developing self-awareness, which is essential for leaders since it enables them to see their advantages, disadvantages, and biases. This information may assist leaders in making better judgments and taking actions consistent with their beliefs and objectives.

Self-advantages reflections for successful leadership include:

Effective leadership may benefit from self-reflection in several ways, including:

Better decision-making: Self-reflection enables leaders to consider many viewpoints and analyze the repercussions of their choices. This leads to better decision-making.

Enhanced self-awareness: Self-reflection enables leaders to understand their assets and liabilities better, allowing them to play to their advantage and strengthen their flaws.

Improved relationships: By self-reflection, leaders may develop greater connections with others by displaying empathy and understanding.

Better problem-solving: Self-reflection aids leaders in approaching issues with an open mind and a clear head, helping them develop creative and practical solutions.

Self-reflection examples for leaders

The capacity to continuously evaluate one's actions and judgments is a trait of effective leaders. As an illustration of how self-reflection may be used in leadership, consider the following:

- Leaders may consider prior events and note what lessons they have gained from them by reflecting. They may apply these lessons to new circumstances with this introspection.
- *Feedback-seeking:* Leaders may ask for feedback from peers, subordinates, and superiors to understand their strengths and faults better.
- *Finding areas for development:* Self-reflection helps leaders pinpoint the areas where they need to enhance their abilities. Then, via training and development, leaders may address these issues.
- *Goal-setting:* Self-reflection aids leaders in establishing objectives that are consistent with their beliefs and aspirations. Then, leaders may utilize

these objectives to direct their decisions and deeds.

Self-reflection is an important quality for good leadership. It helps people become more self-aware, improve their choices, and forge greater bonds with others. Leaders may find areas for development and take action to realize their full leadership potential by regularly reflecting on their actions and choices.

2.2 Self Evaluation

Self-evaluation is a vital component of successful leadership growth. Reflecting on one's performance and actions allow leaders to pinpoint their strong and weak points and improve. Self-assessment tools provide leaders unbiased feedback on their leadership philosophies, practices, and effectiveness. The numerous self-assessment techniques that may be used to evaluate oneself and improve one's leadership abilities are covered in this section.

360-Degree Evaluation

360-degree feedback is one of the most often utilized self-assessment techniques. This tool gathers input from the leader, their peers, subordinates, and superiors, among other sources. The anonymous feedback is gathered to give the leader a complete picture of their performance and leadership style. The feedback may identify the leader's leadership strengths and areas for development, providing a comprehensive picture of the leader's capabilities.

Personality evaluations

Personality tests are another self-evaluation technique that might be helpful for leaders. These evaluations examine a leader's personality attributes and show how they affect their leadership approach. The Myers-Briggs Type Indicator (MBTI), for instance, may assist leaders in understanding their personality type and how it affects their communication style, decision-making process, and ability to resolve conflict.

The Influence of Personality Exams

There are several scenarios in which personality testing is helpful. The results of these examinations might shed light on your character strengths and flaws. Although the results of each personality test will be unique, discovering that you score highly on a certain attribute might provide light on your habits and motivations.

Personality tests may provide interesting insights about oneself, such as how much one grades on the introversion scale. This finding shows that engaging with others requires effort, so it's important to schedule time alone to refuel. By being aware of this trait, you may take steps to prevent social exhaustion and restore your energy.

How to Ace Your Next Personality Test

While you can't train yourself to perform well on a personality test, there are steps you can take to ensure that your scores are an accurate picture of who you are:

- Honesty is required. It would help if you didn't pretend to be someone you're not.

Try to respond in a manner that is authentic to who you are and how you feel.

- Have a read-through of the manual. If you cannot follow the instructions or answer the questions correctly, your findings may not represent who you really are.
- Never attempt to "cram for the exam." Do not attempt to second-guess what the "correct" response could be. Be sincere in your response.

Looking around at the many personality tests, one thing will likely stand out immediately: many are classified as "informal." There are a plethora of online tests and quizzes that claim to reveal some aspect of your character with only a few clicks. The bulk of quizzes you'll find online are only for amusement. They're not rigorous, scientific examinations of character, but they may be fun and provide you with some insight into who you are.

Challenges That May Arise

Personality tests may be informative in certain situations, but it doesn't imply they are risk-free.

You Can Easily Be Duped

One major drawback of self-report inventories is that respondents could lie about their answers. People frequently provide misleading responses in an attempt to "fake good" or look more socially acceptable and desired, even though procedures may be used to identify dishonesty.

It's Time to Look within

Individuals' limited ability to objectively describe their actions is another possible hurdle. Humans are biased towards exaggerating the importance of certain traits while downplaying the importance of others, particularly those held in higher esteem by society. As a result, the reliability of a personality assessment may suffer.

Self-report personality tests may also be lengthy, requiring several hours in certain circumstances. It's easy to see why some people could become annoyed and bored. Examinees rush through their responses in these situations, often without reading the questions.

Scoring Methods May Be Flawed

There are a few drawbacks and restrictions to projective testing as well. The first difficulty arises when trying to make sense of the data. Examinees' answers may be interpreted differently depending on the rater since item scoring is extremely subjective.

There's a Chance of Varying Outcomes

Unfortunately, not all tests of human character may be trusted. Consistency in results is what we mean by "reliability," whereas "validity" refers to whether or not the test measures what it claims to.

Leadership Style Evaluations

Assessments of a person's leadership style may be useful tools for self-evaluation. These evaluations examine a leader's chosen leadership style and provide advice on adjusting to various circumstances. The Situational Leadership Model, for instance, evaluates a leader's adaptability to change their leadership style according to the demands of their team or scenario.

Assessments of emotional intelligence

Assessments of emotional intelligence (EI) may be helpful for leaders. These tests measure a leader's capacity for self-awareness and emotional control over their emotions and those of others. Leaders with high EI can better establish rapport, handle disputes, and communicate clearly. One EI assessment instrument that might assist leaders in honing their emotional intelligence abilities is the Emotional Quotient Inventory (EQ-i).

Exercises for Self-Reflection

These activities help leaders evaluate their past experiences, habits, and actions to pinpoint areas that need change. Exercises that promote self-reflection include writing, meditation, and discussion groups.

Name: _____ Date: _____

My Visual Journal

Read the prompts below and respond by filling each space provided with images and words that come into mind.

The best things that happened today:	Things I wish I can change about today:

I am proud of myself today because...	I think I still need to work on....

Self-Assessment Tools' Advantages

Tools for self-assessment are quite helpful for leaders who desire to develop their leadership abilities. Some of the main advantages are as follows:

Self-assessment tools provide leaders with unbiased feedback on their performance and leadership philosophies. Leaders may use this feedback to pinpoint their strong and weak points and create improvement strategies. Self-assessment techniques may aid leaders in developing their self-awareness. Leaders may better understand their strengths, shortcomings, and leadership style by taking stock of their actions and performance.

They help leaders make better judgments because they provide them with more information. Leaders may make better-informed judgments consistent with their beliefs and objectives by knowing their leadership style, personality characteristics, and emotional intelligence. Improved connections: Strong relationships with team members, stakeholders, and others are essential for effective leadership. Self-assessment tools may assist leaders in improving their relationship-building abilities and emotional intelligence.

They may be quite effective for leaders who desire to develop their leadership abilities. Leaders may learn a lot about their performance and behaviors by utilizing tools like 360-degree feedback, personality tests, leadership style tests, emotional intelligence tests, and self-reflection activities. These techniques aid a leader's self-awareness, decision-making, and relationship-building with their team and stakeholders.

2.3 Developing self-confidence and a positive self-image

Positive self-talk is one of many skills and attitudes that effective leaders must possess. Reframing negative ideas into more positive ones with the positive self-talk approach boosts one's resilience and self-confidence. This chapter will discuss the advantages of positive self-talk as a quality of good leadership. We will also provide examples of how constructive self-talk may be used in various leadership contexts.

Positive self-talk

You may be engaging in self-talk if you constantly criticize yourself. Your unconscious mind has a hand in it and discloses your innermost sentiments, ideas, questions, and speculations.

Both good and negative self-talk exist. The results might be both uplifting and disheartening. Your personality influences how much you speak to yourself. Your internal monologue may be more upbeat and optimistic if you're a positive person If you're typically a pessimist, you'll find the contrary true. Optimism and a positive outlook may be helpful stress relievers. Furthermore, health advantages are associated with adopting a more optimistic attitude toward life. For example, research from 2010 found that optimists tend to live longer.

With positive self-talk, one may replace negative self-talk with uplifting phrases. The process includes affirmations, constructive self-criticism, and turning negative ideas into good ones. Enhancing self-esteem, increasing confidence, and cultivating a more optimistic attitude are the objectives of positive self-talk.

Positive self-talk has advantages for leaders:

Successful leaders often employ positive self-talk to overcome challenges, stay focused on their objectives, and have a positive outlook. Positive self-talk has several advantages for leaders, including:

- Positive self-talk may assist leaders in overcoming self-doubt and pessimistic thoughts. Leaders may boost their confidence and take on bigger tasks by repeating positive attitudes about themselves and their capabilities.
- Positive self-talk strengthens leaders' resilience, making them more capable of overcoming obstacles. They are more

prone to see challenges as passing things and can better resolve issues.

- Leaders may communicate more effectively by encouraging self-talk. Leaders may inspire and encourage their people by keeping a good outlook and speaking positively.
- Good self-talk may assist leaders in maintaining focus and producing superior judgments. Leaders are better able to think clearly and come up with original ideas when challenges are presented favorably.

Positive self-talk examples in leadership:

Affirmations: Leaders may use affirmations to reaffirm their self-confidence and competence. A leader could tell themself, for instance, "I can handle any issue that comes my way."

Constructive self-criticism: It is a tool leaders may use to enhance their performance. A leader may tell themself, for instance, "I should have handled that scenario better, but I will learn from my errors and do better next time."

Positive thinking reframing: Leaders may transform negative ideas into constructive ones. For instance, a leader could tell oneself that a challenging situation is a chance for learning and growth and that they can come up with a solution.

Leaders may employ visualization to see themselves accomplishing their objectives. For instance, a leader could see herself making a compelling presentation or inspiring their team to an important victory.

In short, positive self-talk is a strong technique for developing the self-belief, resiliency, and optimistic outlook required for successful leadership. Leaders may inspire and encourage their employees and overcome challenges with a positive mindset by employing positive self-talk strategies. Positive self-talk is a feature of successful leadership that may be fostered and exercised to enhance leadership abilities and achieve more success.

How do affirmations work?

Positive words, known as affirmations, are ones people repeat to themselves to maintain a good outlook and increase confidence.

Name_ _ _ _ _ _ _ _ _ _ _ _ _ _ _ _

Classroom Affirmations

We are going to create a classroom Affirmation Station
on our wall. Please write down your favorite positive
affirmations and we will cut them out and put them
on our wall.

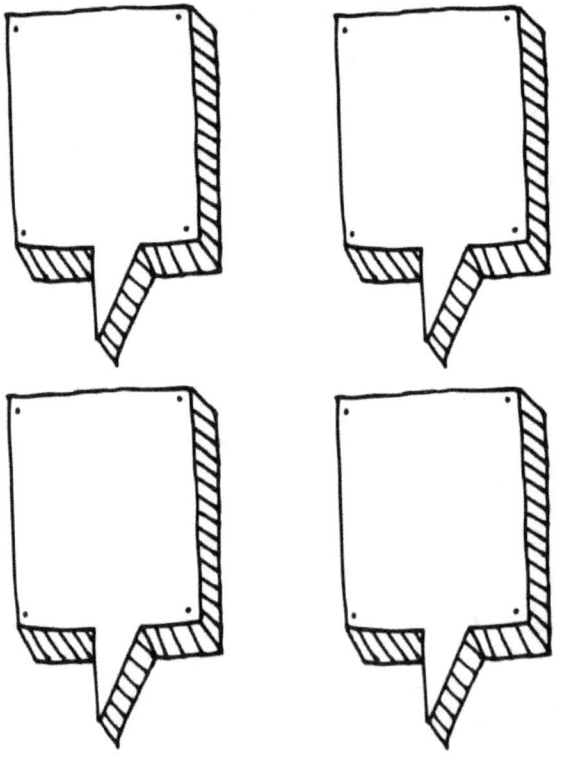

The important thing is that they should be individualized and relevant to the person. These statements might be simple or complicated. Affirmations aim to develop a positive self-image that aids in overcoming negative thoughts and self-doubt.

Significance of Affirmations in Leadership

Being a leader may be difficult where self-doubt and unfavorable ideas can seep in, making it difficult for a leader to make choices and motivate others. This is where affirmations may be really helpful. A leader may develop optimism and resilience by concentrating on positive remarks, which can help them deal with failures and motivate others.

Affirmations that may foster successful leadership skills include the following:

- I am a self-assured and competent leader with faith in my talents and gut feelings.
- As a leader, I am open to criticism and always learn new things.

- I have strong communication skills; I actively listen and convey information efficiently.
- I am a creative and tenacious problem-solver who approaches difficulties head-on.
- I positively impact my team, and I motivate them to do their best work.
- I have a strong sense of purpose and motivation and strive fervently and relentlessly to accomplish my objectives.
- My team and others around me are important because I am a caring leader.

Applying Affirmations in Everyday Life

There are several methods to employ affirmations depending on personal preferences. Affirmations may be said loudly, written down, or repeated to oneself in front of a mirror, depending on the person. Whichever approach is used, the most important thing is to integrate affirmations into everyday living. Regular affirmation should be repeated to establish good habits and support a positive mentality. Consistency is crucial.

In short, affirmations may be useful for cultivating the required attributes and qualities of strong leaders, which are crucial in both personal and professional situations. Leaders may cultivate a positive outlook, increase their confidence, and motivate others to succeed by adding affirmations into their everyday lives. Affirmations are simple but effective techniques that may significantly improve a leader's performance.

2.4 Visualization Technique

Imagination, creativity, and mental images may all be improved via visualization. It is a potent tool that may be used in various contexts, including business, sports, and personal growth. Making a mental image of a desired goal to accelerate its reality is known as visualization. Visualization may help with goal-setting, problem-solving, and decision-making in leadership. The advantages of visualizing as a leadership quality and the methods for developing it will be covered in this chapter.

The advantages of visualization as a leadership quality

There are several advantages of Visualization technique:

Enhancing Decision Making:

Visualization aids in decision-making by assisting leaders in defining their aims and objectives. A leader may understand the possible effects of their choices and choose the best course of action to reach their objectives by picturing the intended result.

Superior Problem-Solving

Leaders may choose the best strategy to solve a problem by visualizing the issue and alternative solutions. Thanks to this approach, they can think creatively and explore many options, which produces better answers.

Enhancing Goal Setting

A great strategy for establishing and attaining objectives is visualization. A leader may generate a clear mental image of the result they want to attain by visualizing it, which makes it simpler to formulate a strategy and take action to get there.

How to Build the Leadership Attribute of Visualization

You can build attribute of visualization by following these strategies:

Practice

Practice is the key to mastering the art of visualization. Taking a few minutes each day to imagine a desired result or objective might be a good place for leaders to start. They may gradually add other situations and elements to their visualizations to make them more sophisticated.

Usage of Imagery Leaders may utilize imagery to conjure up crystal-clear, vivid images in their heads. They may add all the senses, including touch, taste, and smell, to make the vision lifelike.

Restorative Practices

Deep breathing, meditation, and yoga are all relaxation practices that may assist leaders in achieving a level of calm and clarity that improves visualization. Imagining and envisaging the desired result when the mind is calm is simpler.

Positivity in Oneself

Visualization may be improved by using positive self-talk to cultivate a positive mentality. Affirmations and encouraging self-talk may help leaders strengthen their vision and develop confidence in their capacity to succeed.

Examples of Leadership Visualization

Setting goals

An effective strategy for achieving a goal is to visualize it. For instance, a manager who wishes to boost sales might see the actions they must take, such as finding new markets, creating new goods, and enhancing customer service.

Making Decisions

A leader can make the optimal choice by visualizing the possible consequences. A leader, for instance, can see a project's possible risks and advantages to make an educated choice about whether to invest in it.

Fixing issues

A leader may choose the optimal strategy for tackling an issue by visualizing it and alternative solutions. For instance, a crisis-affected leader might see many situations and their possible results to decide on the best action.

Enhancing one's imagination, creativity, and mental images can be done by using visualization. Leadership may use it to enhance goal-setting, problem-solving, and decision-making. Leaders may see their objectives clearly and take action to reach them by adding visualization to their leadership style. Leaders may acquire this quality and boost their efficacy by practicing relaxation methods, encouraging self-talk, and using imagery.

2.5 Learning to manage emotions and handle stress

Emotional intelligence, or EQ, is the capacity to recognize, comprehend, and control one's emotions and those of others. Emotional intelligence is critical for great leaders because it helps them communicate, establish lasting bonds with others, and make wise judgments. This chapter will discuss the many facets of emotional intelligence and how they support successful leadership.

Self-Awareness

The basis of emotional intelligence is self-awareness. It entails being able to identify and comprehend one's own emotions as well as the effects they have on others. Self-aware leaders can better control their emotions and react properly to various circumstances. For instance, if a leader is aware that they often get furious when receiving criticism, they may try to control this reaction, such as pausing to think before reacting.

Self-Regulation

A person's capacity to restrain their emotions and impulses is called self-regulation. It entails the capacity to deliberate before acting, to withstand pressure, and to adjust to shifting conditions. A leader with self-control can better maintain composure under pressure, which is necessary for successful leadership. For instance, when a leader must make a tough choice, they may utilize self-regulation to weigh their choices before deciding.

Motivation

A person's desire to accomplish their objectives is referred to as motivation. A motivated leader may energize and excite their team to accomplish shared objectives. They may also have an optimistic outlook despite trying situations. For instance, a leader driven to accomplish a certain objective may urge their team to go towards that goal even when they face obstacles.

Empathy

The capacity to comprehend and relate to the emotions of others is referred to as empathy. Empathic leaders can better connect with their team members because they can comprehend their viewpoints and react accordingly. Also, they possess strong communication skills, which are crucial for successful leadership. An empathic leader will, for instance, take the time to understand a team member's viewpoint if they are having difficulty with a specific job and will then give support and direction.

Social abilities

"Social skills" refers to a person's capacity for clear communication, solid interpersonal bonds, and teamwork. Strong social skills enable leaders to convey their vision and motivate their team to collaborate on a shared objective. Also, they possess the conflict-resolution and negotiation skills necessary for successful leadership. For instance, leaders with good social skills may establish enduring bonds with their team members and foster a productive workplace.

Emotional intelligence is only one of many skills and abilities that effective leaders must possess. Emotionally intelligent leaders can better control their emotions, establish lasting bonds with others, and make wise choices. Leaders may enhance their effectiveness in their professions and motivate their teams to succeed by mastering emotional intelligence.

With strength and bravery, leadership positions also call for resilience, the capacity to deal with stress, and the capability to face challenging circumstances. Successful leaders can handle stress and maintain composure under pressure, enabling them to make judgments objectively in even the most trying situations. This chapter examines the coping mechanisms used by successful leaders to control stress and triumph over adversity.

Coping Mechanism

Coping mechanisms are how people deal with stress, anxiety, and other unpleasant feelings. To manage the emotional effects of stress without necessarily fixing the problem, coping methods may either be a problem- or emotion-focused. Problem-focused coping involves taking steps to address the issue that is producing stress. To negotiate difficult circumstances, effective leaders use problem-focused and emotion-focused coping mechanisms.

Illustrations of coping mechanisms

- Successful leaders are aware of the significance of time management in lowering stress. Leaders may reduce the possibility of feeling overburdened by their job by setting priorities and using time management techniques efficiently.
- Leaders who want to relax their thoughts and concentrate on the here and now utilize mindfulness and meditation as tools. These techniques assist leaders in staying focused and avoiding distractions when faced with stress and difficulty.
- Exercise has significantly lowered stress levels and enhanced mental health. To improve their mood and strengthen their resilience, many leaders regularly exercise.
- Leaders know that they cannot handle all issues independently. People seek assistance from coworkers, mentors, and

reliable people to share their difficulties and acquire fresh viewpoints on difficult circumstances.

- Leaders with positive self-talk have superior stress management and self-confidence skills. Leaders may increase their confidence and resilience by rephrasing negative ideas more positively.

- Leaders utilize humor as a potent coping mechanism to defuse difficult circumstances and lighten the atmosphere. Leaders may lower stress and foster a more pleasant work atmosphere by finding comedy in challenging situations.

- Successful leaders recognize that errors are a necessary component of the learning process. Leaders utilize failures as chances for development and learning, not a reason to give up.

Successful leaders must control their stress levels and maintain their composure under pressure. Coping mechanisms are crucial for helping leaders manage the difficulties of their positions and keep their mental health in check. Leaders may increase their resilience, improve their decision-making ability, and ultimately become more successful by implementing problem-focused and emotion-focused coping mechanisms into their daily routines.

2.6 Mindfulness & Meditation

It is simple to become lost in the turmoil of daily living in today's fast-paced world. Leaders who practice mindfulness have a distinct edge because they can maintain their composure and presence no matter what happens around them. Being present and conscious of one's thoughts, emotions, and environment is known as mindfulness. Leaders practicing mindfulness may become more focused, have better decision-making abilities, and experience less stress.

What do mindfulness practices entail?

Practices that foster present-moment awareness and minimize distractions are known as mindfulness methods. These techniques include yoga, body scans, breathing exercises, meditation, and more. They foster positive self-awareness and mental clarity while assisting people in better understanding their feelings and ideas.

How might mindfulness practices benefit leaders?

Leaders who use mindfulness practices might gain from doing so in a variety of ways, including:

- Better decision-making and focus: Mindfulness practices help executives focus on the present, minimizing distractions and boosting productivity. This sharpened attention may help decision-makers make better choices since they can weigh all the information without being distracted by outside influences.
- Decreased stress: Stress may be detrimental to leadership since it can cause burnout, reduced productivity,

and worse decision-making. By encouraging relaxation and lowering emotions of worry, mindfulness practices assist leaders in managing stress.

MINDFULNESS SCAVENGER HUNT

Tick off each activity as you achieve it!

	Watch a sunrise or sunset without taking a photo	Practice deep breathing
Taste something new and describe the flavours 	Colour in a picture	Sit in silence for 20 minutes and listen for hidden sounds 
Feel the different textures of leaves in your garden 	Walk your neighbourhood at dinner time and smell your neighbour's cooking 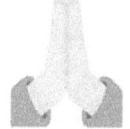	
	Write a list of 10 things you are grateful for	

- Enhanced emotional intelligence: By fostering greater self-awareness and empathy for others, mindfulness practices aid in developing emotional intelligence in leaders. Leaders may better comprehend the emotions of others around them by being in the moment and conscious of their own emotions. This improves communication and teamwork.
- Improved creativity: By encouraging calm and concentration, mindfulness practices aid leaders in accessing their creativity. Eliminating distractions and allowing the mind to roam might help leaders develop fresh, original ideas.

Examples of leadership mindfulness exercises

- Meditation entails sitting quietly, concentrating on the breath, and putting distractions and ideas to rest. Focus may be improved, and tension can be decreased through meditation.

- To encourage relaxation, increase flexibility, and lower stress, yoga combines physical postures, breathing techniques, and meditation.
- Taking slow, deep breaths while concentrating on how the breath feels entering and leaving the body is known as mindful breathing. This may aid in stress reduction and mental calmness.
- A body scan entails paying close attention to each body component, from the toes to the top of the head, and noting any feelings or points of tension. This may lessen tension and help people become more aware of their bodily experiences.
- Giving the speaker your undivided attention without interruption or diversion is mindful listening. Better communication and greater connections may assist.

In conclusion, mindfulness practices are useful tools for leaders who want to increase their emotional intelligence, attention, and decision-making abilities. Leaders may lessen stress, boost creativity, and better understand their emotions and those of others by adding mindfulness activities into their daily routines.

Chapter 3: Communication and Interpersonal Skills

Communication and interpersonal skills are crucial to develop in a teen leader. In this chapter, we will discuss it in detail.

3.1 Developing effective communication skills

Every effective leader must possess the key skill of verbal communication. A leader who can communicate well may express ideas clearly, influence people, and create lasting bonds. The many facets of verbal communication, such as tone, body language, and active listening, will be covered in this chapter.

Verbal Communication

A key component of successful verbal communication is a leader's tone of voice while speaking. Many emotions, like assurance, joy, and sincerity, may be expressed via voice tonality. A strong leader should speak with clarity, assertiveness, and confidence. They should refrain from speaking in an insulting, dismissive, or hostile manner.

Body Language

A vital component of verbal communication success is body language. The body language of a leader may reveal a lot about their mood and purpose. While speaking to others, a leader should make eye contact and avoid crossing their legs or arms, which might come out as defensive or walled off. Moreover, they should refrain from moving about or seeming disinterested since these behaviors might suggest they are not truly listening to what is being said.

Effective verbal communication requires active listening, which is a crucial component. It entails listening carefully to what the other person is saying and expressing your understanding of their viewpoint. A leader who actively listens to their team members may establish better bonds with them by showing appreciation for their opinions and a keen interest in what they say. Maintaining eye contact, asking questions, and summarizing what the other person has said are all examples of active listening.

Let's look at an instance of a leader who is successfully communicating. Consider a manager in charge of a team gathering where a new project is being discussed. The manager speaks with clarity and assertiveness, which exudes confidence and zeal. They avoid crossing their arms or seeming disinterested and keep excellent eye contact with their team members. By asking questions and summarizing what their team members have stated, the manager also exhibits active listening.

Let's now look at a situation where a leader must communicate successfully. Think about a team leader giving a member of their team some comments. The team leader's defensive demeanor is shown by their crossed arms and dismissive tone of speech. They seem inattentive and make poor eye contact with their teammates. To comprehend their team members' perspectives, the team leader does not actively listen to them or elicit information from them.

In conclusion, verbal communication skills are essential for all effective leaders. It entails speaking eloquently and authoritatively, keeping positive body language, and exhibiting active listening. Effective communicators can express ideas, create lasting connections, and influence others. Leaders may improve their verbal communication abilities to enhance their job effectiveness and boost their professional success.

Non Verbal Communication

Leadership requires effective communication. Your team's capacity to be inspired and influenced by you depends on more than simply what you say. Body language, facial expressions, tone of voice, and other nonverbal clues are all examples of nonverbal communication. The significance of nonverbal communication for successful leadership and ways to enhance it will be discussed in this chapter.

Nonverbal communication is important in leadership because it may affect how people see you and the message you are trying to convey. Successful managers are conscious of their body language and utilize it to communicate their objectives and emotions to their workforce. Nonverbal communication is essential for leadership for the following reasons:

Building rapport and trust with your team is facilitated through nonverbal communication. When you display warm and approachable body language and facial expressions, your employees will find it simpler to trust you and feel more connected to you.

Improves Understanding: By clarifying your vocal information, nonverbal signals may assist in improving comprehension. If you nod your head when giving an employee feedback, it conveys agreement and supports what you are saying.

Nonverbal communication is a powerful tool for expressing feelings. Even if you're not expressing anything directly, your body language, tone of voice, and facial expressions may convey your feelings.

Examples of Leadership Nonverbal Communication

These are some examples of nonverbal cues that good leaders use while speaking with their team:

- Keeping eye contact is essential for effective nonverbal communication. It demonstrates that you are alert, engaged, and involved in the other person's words. Leaders that are effective use eye contact to demonstrate their honesty and reliability.
- How you feel may be read a lot from your facial expressions. A frown might imply disapproval or disappointment,

while a grin can suggest friendliness and approachability. Aware of their facial expressions, effective leaders utilize them to reflect their feelings and goals.

- Body Language: Your posture, gestures, and body language may convey confidence and authority. Slouching might project a lack of confidence while standing erect and with your shoulders back. Successful leaders communicate their confidence and authority via their body language.

- Vocal Tone: How you talk might reveal your feelings and attitude towards the person you speak to. Although a loud tone might indicate annoyance or impatience, a soft, soothing tone can show warmth and understanding. Successful leaders are conscious of their voice tone and know how to express their feelings and objectives.

Enhancing Nonverbal Communication

Self-awareness and practice are necessary to enhance nonverbal communication. Here are some pointers to help you communicate better nonverbally:

- Becoming conscious of your nonverbal communication is the first step to enhancing it. Take attention to your nonverbal indicators, such as tone of voice, body language, and facial expressions.
- Employ active listening, which focuses entirely on the person you are communicating with. It conveys your attention and engagement with what they are saying. Active listening is a skill that effective leaders use to enhance their nonverbal communication.
- You may improve your awareness of nonverbal communication by practicing in front of a mirror. You can see how you come across and make changes as necessary.
- Request input from your group or a reliable coworker. They may provide insightful information about how your nonverbal communication is perceived.

In summary, strong leadership is essential to the success of every business. Vision, honesty, empathy, confidence, resilience, and other traits and attributes are only a few examples of the many characteristics that make it up.

We have also talked about how self-awareness, tools for self-evaluation, encouraging self-talk, affirmations, visualization, emotional intelligence, coping mechanisms, mindfulness practices, and verbal and nonverbal communication skills can help you develop and improve these traits and qualities. We may become more successful leaders in our professional and personal lives by comprehending and putting these characteristics and attributes into practice. We hope this book has given readers insightful knowledge and useful tools to help them develop their leadership skills and achieve greater success.

Active Listening

Successful leadership depends on good communication, and active listening is one of the important elements of effective communication. Leaders' strong, active listening abilities increase their capacity to forge lasting bonds, promote trust, and cultivate a productive workplace. This chapter will discuss the significance of active listening and how it may help leaders in different situations.

Active listening involves paying close attention to and comprehending the speaker's message. It requires listening to what is said and observing the speaker's body language, voice tone, and overall message. Active listening calls for the listener to focus on the speaker and remove all other distractions.

Why is Active Listening Essential for Successful Leadership?

For various reasons, successful leadership requires the ability to listen actively. Beginning with respect and understanding for others and active listening. Actively listening by a leader demonstrates that they appreciate their workforce's thoughts, ideas, and concerns.

This increases trust and promotes a productive workplace.

The second benefit of active listening is that it helps leaders better comprehend the requirements, motives, and viewpoints of their workforce. Leaders may build better judgments and problem-solving strategies using this knowledge.

Finally, listening actively encourages productive dialogue. Leaders may improve communication and produce better results by actively listening. By doing so, they can clear up misconceptions, pose questions, and provide suitable responses.

How Can I Become Better at Active Listening?

Practice and effort are needed to improve active listening abilities. Among the strategies to improve active listening abilities are:

- Being present at the moment while avoiding distractions like mobile phones or other technologies is crucial.

- The key to interpreting the speaker's message is to pay close attention to their body language, tone, and overall message.
- Put Oneself in the Speaker's Shoes: To demonstrate empathy, one must attempt to grasp the speaker's point of view.
- Explain Misunderstandings: It's crucial to clarify misinterpretations so that the audience fully comprehends the speaker's message.
- Provide Feedback: Giving feedback to the speaker demonstrates interest in and active engagement with what they are saying.

Active listening in leadership examples:
When an employee approaches a leader with an issue, the leader may utilize active listening techniques by putting aside other distractions and giving the employee's worries their full attention. A team leader may employ active listening during a meeting by asking questions to clarify what the team members are saying and summarizing their thoughts.

To guarantee that the employee's concerns are fully conveyed while providing feedback, a leader might practice active listening by repeating them and expressing empathy in return.

Strong communication skills are necessary for effective leadership, and active listening is crucial to effective communication. Active listening by leaders fosters respect, empathy, and trust, which improves the working environment. Active listening must be honed through practice, effort, and a readiness to be completely present. Leaders may improve their communication skills and become more successful by adding active listening techniques into their leadership style.

3.2 Explaining Non-verbal Communication

Unconsciously employed body language is a potent communication tool. Successful leaders utilize their body language to convey confidence, approachability, and authority because they recognize the value of nonverbal cues. This chapter will examine how body language affects the efficacy of leadership and provide examples of how executives may make the most of their body language.

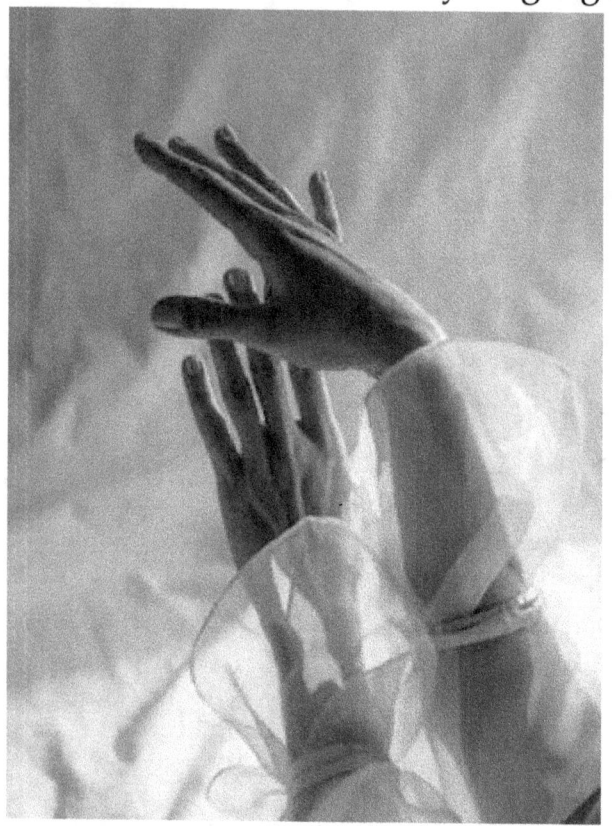

Using physical clues to communicate, such as facial expressions, gestures, and postures, are known as body language. It may express various emotions and attitudes and is often employed subconsciously. Leaders that are aware of body language are better able to understand the body language of others and communicate with their teams.

Good posture is important for leaders, whether standing or sitting down, since it conveys confidence and authority. A lack of confidence or authority may be shown by slouching or hunching over. Also, a leader's posture might convey how approachable they are. Standing with your knees together and your arms at your sides might convey openness, whereas standing with your legs apart and your arms crossed can convey defensiveness.

You may stress points and show emotion using gestures. Successful leaders avoid anxious or fidgety motions, which may be distracting, and only sometimes employ gestures. They also pay close attention to other people's gestures to understand the speaker's emotions and attitudes.

A key method for expressing emotions and attitudes is using facial expressions. Successful leaders demonstrate curiosity, empathy, and understanding via their facial expressions. Smiling effectively establishes a connection and conveys optimism, but frowning or scowling might convey negativity or disdain. Keeping eye contact is a crucial component of successful communication. It exudes curiosity, focus, and assurance. Successful leaders avoid glancing away from the discussion, picking up their phones, or watching while speaking or listening. They also maintain eye contact.

Examples of Effective Body Language

The following are some instances of effective body language that may improve the effectiveness of leadership communication:

- Stand or sit straight when you first meet someone and make eye contact.
- Use hand gestures to highlight crucial ideas, but refrain from making too many or distracting ones.
- To show interest and agreement, smile and nod.
- To seem approachable, keep your posture open and carefree.

- Lean in a little to show that you are interested and engaged.
- To develop rapport and a connection, mimic the other person's body language.

In conclusion, effective leaders know the value of nonverbal cues and use them in their body language to convey authority, approachability, and confidence. Leaders that are aware of body language are better able to understand the body language of others and communicate with their teams. Leaders may increase their effectiveness by developing rapport, establishing trust, and employing good body language.

Facial Expressions

Recognizing and accurately interpreting facial expressions are key skills for leaders who want to communicate nonverbally effectively. Facial expressions are very important in communicating feelings, ideas, and attitudes, which may greatly influence relationships and interpersonal communication. In this chapter, we will examine the significance of facial expressions as a characteristic of good leaders and how they may be used to improve communication and leadership abilities.

The numerous movements and postures of the facial muscles that convey emotions, attitudes, and intentions are referred to as facial expressions. Certain universal facial emotions, such as pleasure, sorrow, anger, surprise, fear, and disgust, are generally recognized across cultures, even though different cultures and people may have different facial expressions. Effective communication depends on accurately comprehending these expressions since they reveal the speaker's feelings, ideas, and intentions.

Significance of Facial Expressions in Leadership

Facial expressions are very important because they may indicate assurance, dependability, empathy, and other crucial traits for successful leadership. Successful leaders inspire, encourage, and connect with followers through facial expressions. They can manage their emotions, project confidence, and leave a good impression on others by being mindful of their facial expressions. Moreover, facial expressions may assist leaders in developing the crucial leadership qualities of rapport and trust with their followers.

Examples of Facial Expressions in Leadership

There are several instances when facial expressions have a negative influence on leadership. For instance, a leader who smiles regularly might create a friendly environment that makes their followers feel at ease and encourages conversation. A boss who frowns or scowls, on the other hand, may foster a hostile environment that obstructs collaboration and production.

A competent leader may inspire confidence in their followers amid a crisis by displaying a calm and comforting look instead of a scared or nervous expression, which might spread disorder and terror among the followers. Similarly, a leader's facial expressions during negotiations or meetings may indicate their objectives and emotions, assisting them in establishing credibility and influence.

Knowledge of one's facial expressions and understanding how it affects leadership and communication is essential for effective leaders. Developing facial expression awareness might require practicing mindfulness and self-reflection to recognize repetitive expressions and emotions that could impede communication or harm leadership. Using video feedback to watch one's facial expressions during presentations or discussions is one way to increase facial expression awareness. This method may assist in pinpointing problem areas and provide insight into how to utilize facial expressions to improve leadership and communication.

Effective leaders must recognize and understand facial expressions, which are crucial to nonverbal communication. Leaders may utilize their facial expressions to communicate confidence, trustworthiness, empathy, and other crucial traits required for successful leadership by being aware of them and knowing how they affect communication and leadership. Face expression awareness may be developed via self-reflection, mindfulness, and tools like video feedback to enhance communication and leadership abilities.

Tone of Voice

Poor communication is a fundamental impediment to successful leadership. A key component of communication that may impact how messages are understood and received is voice tone. The way others see a leader and the message they are attempting to express may be greatly influenced by their tone of voice. In this chapter, we will discuss the significance of voice tone in successful leadership and provide examples of how to utilize voice tone to improve communication.

The tone of one's voice is a crucial component of nonverbal communication since it reveals a person's attitude, mood, and purpose. It could affect how information is taken in and understood. Leaders must be conscious of their tone to guarantee clear communication and prevent misunderstandings.

The following are some justifications for why vocal tone is important in leadership:

- Building Authority: The tone of a leader's voice is very important in doing this. Leaders should establish their authority and position of power by speaking in a clear tone. A weak or unsure tone might cause people to question a leader's authority.
- Developing rapport: Leaders may foster a good, approachable atmosphere among their team members. It may encourage free communication among team members, which can contribute to developing trust.
- Conveying Emotion: A variety of emotions, such as joy, rage, irritation, and disappointment, may be expressed by voice tone. Effective leaders must use the right tone to express the message they are attempting to get through.

Examples of how to use a tone of voice while leading:

The following are some instances of good leadership using voice tone:

- Giving Feedback: To prevent the worsening of the issue, leaders must provide feedback in a neutral, calm manner. Team members may become defensive and resistant to feedback if you use a harsh or critical tone.
- When assigning duties to team members, leaders should speak authoritatively and confidently. It may communicate the task's significance and inspire the team to finish it effectively.
- Supporting Team Members: Leaders may help team members emotionally by speaking in a kind and sympathetic manner. It may increase morale and work satisfaction by making team members feel heard and understood.

In conclusion, voice tone is a crucial component of successful leadership. To successfully communicate their message, leaders must be conscious of their voice tone and employ it correctly. A leader's authority can be established, relationships with the team may be cultivated, and emotions can be correctly expressed via tone of voice. Successful leaders use a variety of tones depending on the circumstance and message they are attempting to deliver. Leaders may enhance communication and create a more productive and happy work environment by successfully employing a tone of voice.

3.3 Building relationships and working with others

A successful leader must possess some crucial traits, including empathy. It is the capacity to empathize with and share the emotions of others. It is crucial for forming connections, speaking clearly, and fostering a supportive work atmosphere. The significance of empathy for successful leadership will be discussed in this chapter, along with techniques for honing it.

Importance of Empathy for Successful Leadership

Good leaders must have empathy because it enables them to recognize and address the wants and worries of their team members. Empathetic leaders may create solid bonds with their team members, boosting loyalty, engagement, and trust. By encouraging a culture of comprehension, respect, and cooperation, leaders may use empathy to improve the workplace.

Techniques for Fostering Empathy

Empathy is a talent that can be honed with practice and effort. The following tactics may help leaders improve their capacity for empathy:

- Empathy requires active listening, which is a crucial skill. It is listening intently and attempting to grasp the speaker's point of view without passing judgment or interjecting. Leaders that actively listen to their team members may improve communication and create a more productive workplace.

- Perspective-taking: Perspective-taking is the capacity to place oneself in another person's position and see events from that person's point of view. It entails considering their ideas, emotions, and experiences and picturing how you would feel if you were in their shoes. Having a different perspective might help leaders better grasp the wants and concerns of their team members.
- The capacity to understand, control, and regulate both your own and other people's emotions is known as emotional intelligence. It entails being able to read and react to the emotions of others as well as being conscious of your feelings and how they influence your conduct. Leaders that possess emotional intelligence will be better able to recognize and address the needs of their team members.
- Cultural competency is comprehending, valuing, and collaborating well with

individuals from various backgrounds. It entails being conscious of your cultural prejudices and views and being able to interact and work well with individuals from other cultural backgrounds. Culturally competent leaders may foster more positive working relationships and an inclusive workplace.

Examples of Empathetic Leadership

Empathetic leadership is shown often. Abraham Lincoln, renowned for his capacity for empathy, is one of the most well-known instances. Lincoln visited with troops and their families during the Civil War to hear their concerns and tales. He also treated his political rivals respectfully and tried to comprehend their viewpoints.

Satya Nadella, CEO of Microsoft, is another illustration of compassionate leadership. With his leadership style, Nadella has highlighted the value of empathy and has prompted his team to concentrate on comprehending the requirements and problems of their clients.

Also, he has improved the workplace climate by supporting Microsoft's diversity and inclusion programs.

The ability to empathize is crucial for good leadership, in sum. It enables leaders to forge closer connections with their team members, address their wants and problems, and foster a more productive atmosphere. To develop empathy, active listening, perspective-taking, emotional intelligence, and cultural competency. Leaders may improve their capacity for empathy and become more successful by honing these abilities.

Examining the characteristics and attributes of successful leaders

- Settlement of Conflict

Conflict often happens at work and is an inherent aspect of life. For a leader to maintain a happy and effective workplace, it is essential to learn conflict resolution techniques. Good conflict-resolution techniques encourage cooperation and creativity within a team and minimize negative effects. This section will examine successful conflict-resolution leaders' characteristics and attributes.

Good communication is one of the key characteristics of a successful leader in conflict resolution. To grasp the underlying reason for the disagreement, leaders must be able to express themselves effectively, actively listen to others' viewpoints, and show empathy. To resolve issues, it is also crucial to discourage forming assumptions and promote open communication. Another essential quality for successful conflict resolution is empathy.

Leaders should be able to put themselves in others' shoes and comprehend their viewpoints. Empathy enables leaders to connect with their team, foster trust, and resolve conflicts in original ways.

Strong problem-solving abilities enable leaders to identify and successfully address the underlying causes of a disagreement. They can assess the situation, acquire data, and develop a strategy to fix the problem. Critical, unbiased, and creative thinking are also necessary for developing strong problem-solving abilities.

Negotiation Skills: Effective leaders must be able to negotiate to reach amicable resolutions to conflicts. Strong negotiators can identify the needs and preferences of both parties and come to an agreement that benefits them both. Effective communication, active listening, and empathy are necessary for good bargaining abilities.

Patience is a key quality for successful dispute resolution. Even when dealing with problematic team members or difficult events, leaders should be able to maintain their composure and patience while handling disputes. Leaders must also know that resolving conflicts may take time and requires constant cooperation and communication.

Consider a scenario where a team member consistently misses deadlines, resulting in tension and disagreement. A leader with excellent conflict resolution skills would first listen to the team member's explanations for missing deadlines to assist and resolve any underlying problems. The team member and the leader would then develop a schedule for meeting deadlines while ensuring the team member's workload is reasonable.

Another example is when two team members have different approaches to a project. An effective leader would promote open communication among the team members so that everyone could comprehend the other's viewpoints and devise a solution that considers both. The leader could also consult with other team members to develop a unique solution that works for the whole team.

To maintain a healthy and productive work environment, leaders must have the ability to resolve conflicts. The ability to effectively communicate, empathize, solve problems, negotiate, and have patience are essential for conflict resolution. Leaders may encourage team creativity and cooperation and create a healthy workplace culture by mastering these skills and attributes.

Chapter 4: Goal-Setting and Time Management

Setting and achieving objectives is one of the essential characteristics of a successful leader. Setting goals is vital, but ensuring they're SMART objectives is crucial. Specific, Measurable, Achievable, Relevant, and Time-bound are all acronyms for SMART goals. This chapter will discuss the significance of creating SMART objectives and how doing so may aid in a leader's performance.

Specificity: A SMART objective should be precise as its initial attribute. This implies that it must be distinct and well-defined, with no space for ambiguity. For instance, if a leader wishes to boost the company's sales, a particular objective would be to raise revenue by 20% in the next quarter. This objective is specific and quantifiable, so monitoring progress and spotting problem areas are simpler.

Measurable: A SMART objective must meet the second requirement to be quantifiable. This implies that the goal's progress should be straightforward to measure. For instance, if a leader wishes to raise customer satisfaction, a quantifiable target would be to do so by 10% for the next six months. Monitoring the goal's progress helps track accomplishments and gives a feeling of satisfaction.

Achievable: A SMART goal's third quality is that it must be reachable. This suggests that the objective should be easy to attain but attainable. A leader may need help to achieve the target of boosting sales by 500% in the next month, for instance. Establishing impossible objectives might cause team members to become frustrated and unmotivated. Setting difficult yet reasonable and reachable objectives is crucial.

Relevant: A SMART goal's fourth quality must be relevant. This indicates the target should align with the organization's broader vision and goals. A comparable aim might be to expand market share by 10% during the next year, for instance, if the company aims to increase market share. The team's efforts will align with the business's general direction if appropriate objectives are set.

Time-bound: A SMART objective should be time-bound as its last attribute. This indicates that the objective should have a deadline for completion. For instance, if a leader wants to reduce staff turnover, a time-bound aim would be to do so by 20% over the next six months. Establishing a deadline instills a feeling of urgency and concentrates efforts on accomplishing the objective.

Examples of SMART objectives
- Increasing the client base via focused marketing initiatives may boost revenues by 10% in the next quarter.
- Over the following six months, increase staff productivity by 15% by implementing a new performance management system.

- By improving the organization's advantages, 20% less staff will leave the following year.
- Enhancing customer service training for all staff may raise customer satisfaction levels by 15% in the next quarter.
- You may introduce a new product line within the next year by doing market research and creating a strategic strategy.

In light of the above, setting SMART objectives is an essential leadership skill. SMART goals provide a framework for establishing precise, quantifiable, doable, pertinent, and time-bound objectives that aid in concentrating efforts toward achievement. By adopting SMART objectives, leaders can inspire their teams, monitor progress, and produce better outcomes. So, to promote development and success inside their firms, executives must have this competence.

4.1 Action Planning

It takes rigorous preparation and execution to carry out a project, charm, and a clear vision.

Effective leaders must be able to organize their actions to make their ideas a reality. We will discuss the value of action planning in leadership in this section and how it may support leaders in achieving their objectives.

SMART GOALS

Setting realistic and achievable outcomes.

My goal is:

SPECIFIC	What do I want to happen?	
MEASUREABLE	How will I know when I have achieved my goal?	
ATTAINABLE	Is the goal realistic and how will I accomplish it?	
RELEVANT	Why is my goal important to me?	
TIMELY	What is my deadline for this goal?	

Developing a step-by-step strategy to accomplish a specific objective is known as action planning. It is crucial to leadership because it enables leaders to put their ideas into practice. An action plan lists the steps that must be followed, the materials needed, the deadline for completion, and the person or team in charge of each step.

Action planning is the technique that enables effective leaders to achieve this. Successful leaders must be able to translate their ideas into actions. Many factors make action planning essential for good leadership, including the following:

- Clarity: Action planning makes it simpler for leaders to explain their vision to their team by clarifying the actions necessary to accomplish a goal.
- Accountability: A clear assignment of responsibilities within an action plan makes it simpler to monitor progress and hold people responsible for their actions.
- Prioritization: An action plan helps set priorities for activities and efficiently allocate resources, ensuring that the most important tasks are finished first.

- Flexibility: Leaders may respond to unanticipated obstacles while pursuing their objective by modifying an action plan as conditions change.

Examples of leadership action planning include:

Following are some instances of how leadership uses action planning:

- ❖ Business Strategy: An action plan is a key instrument for creating a company strategy. It describes the steps necessary to achieve the strategy's objectives: marketing, sales, product development, and customer service.
- ❖ An action plan, which outlines the actions necessary to accomplish the project, the timetable, and the resources required, is a crucial component of project management.
- ❖ Personal Development: An action plan that outlines the steps necessary to enhance communication, delegation, and

decision-making may be utilized to build leadership abilities.

❖ Crisis management: During a crisis, an action plan outlining the activities to control the situation and lessen its effects on the company is essential.

Action planning is a crucial leadership ability that enables leaders to translate their vision into reality. An action plan is crucial for reaching objectives in any business because it offers clarity, responsibility, prioritizing, and flexibility. Aspiring leaders should concentrate on honing their action-planning abilities to be more successful in their positions.

4.2 Avoid Procrastination

The practice of putting off important choices or duties is known as procrastination. It is a frequent issue that many leaders deal with, often resulting in lost opportunities, poor productivity, and elevated stress. Time management and avoiding procrastination are important skills for effective leaders. This chapter will examine the characteristics and abilities that procrastination-preventing leaders have.

Successful leaders have many characteristics and abilities that aid them in avoiding procrastination.

Let's go into further depth about a few of these qualities:

- The capacity for self-control over one's behaviors, ideas, and emotions is known as self-discipline. Strong self-control enables effective leaders to concentrate on their objectives and avoid procrastination. They can determine priorities and keep their word even when they don't feel like it.
- Successful leaders are aware of the significance of time management. They assign time to each assignment, prioritize activities, and establish deadlines. They use strategies and tools like calendars, timetables, and to-do lists to keep organized and focused.

- Effective leaders establish clear and attainable objectives. They divide bigger objectives into smaller, more doable activities to prevent feeling overwhelmed. They develop practical and doable objectives using the SMART goal-setting framework (specific, measurable, attainable, relevant, and time-bound).
- Accountability: Successful leaders take ownership of their deeds and choices. They hold themselves to a high level and work hard to achieve it. Also, they take ownership of their errors and work to make amends.
- Focus: Capable leaders can concentrate on their objectives while avoiding distractions. Distractions like social media, emails and phone calls are reduced or eliminated. To retain concentration and prevent burnout, they also use strategies like the Pomodoro Method, which entails working for a certain period before taking a little break.

Instances of Procrastination Avoidance

These are a few instances of excellent leaders that don't procrastinate in their everyday lives:

- Amazon's founder Jeff Bezos has a two-pizza team policy for meetings. In other words, he only invites as many people to a meeting as two pizzas can feed. This keeps meetings on task and cuts down on time wastage.
- The CEO of Tesla and SpaceX, Elon Musk, employs time-blocking to organize his calendar. He plans all of his activities for the day, including breaks and meals, in five-minute intervals. He can maintain organization and goal focus, thanks to this.
- The COO of Meta, Sheryl Sandberg, establishes distinct lines between work and personal life. She leaves work at a decent hour every day to spend time with her family. This allows her to prevent burnout and keep focused on her objectives.

Effective leaders recognize the necessity of time management and preventing procrastination. They have some characteristics and attributes that enable them to concentrate on their objectives and avoid distractions. The qualities of good leaders include self-control, time management, goal-setting, accountability, and focus, to name just a few. You may need to work on completing your objectives by following their lead and using these techniques.

Overcoming procrastination and distractions
Time is crucial in today's fast-paced environment, and great leaders must manage it effectively. Finding personal distractions is a crucial component of efficient time management. This entails identifying the sources of your work-related distractions and taking action to remove or minimize them. In this section, we'll examine the characteristics and skills of successful leaders, including how they recognize and manage personal distractions.

What is private distraction?

Everything that keeps you from finishing your task or reaching your objectives is a personal distraction. These interruptions might be internal — negative thoughts, tension, or lack of focus — or external — noise, interruptions from colleagues or family members. Personal diversion may hinder productivity, leading to missed deadlines, worse quality work, and higher stress levels.

Characteristics and abilities of successful leaders when recognizing personal distractions:

Self-awareness

Successful leaders are conscious of their virtues and shortcomings. They are aware of their distractions and take steps to eliminate them. They take the time to consider their working practices and pinpoint areas that might need better. For example, a manager aware that social media alerts quickly divert them, sets up specified times throughout the day to check their phone and restricts access while at work.

Focus

Even in the presence of distractions, effective leaders can maintain focus on their objectives. They take measures to reduce or remove distractions since they are aware of how they might impede development. Example: A manager who, to reduce distractions, establishes a certain time each day for email answers and disables email alerts while the team is in session.

4.3 Management of time

Successful leaders prioritize their time and ensure enough time to do their tasks. They plan their day's work so that they may control their workload and get rid of any distractions. For example, consider a leader who organizes their day the night before and allots time for breaks and concentrated work to avoid burnout and minimize distractions.

Stress reduction

Successful leaders take measures to control stress because they know how it affects their ability to perform at work. They determine what stresses them out and take action to reduce or remove these stressors.

An example is a leader who recognizes that excessive work causes stress and regularly takes daily breaks to lower stress levels.

Proactivity

Proactively tackling their distraction management is a trait of effective leaders. They prepare for possible distractions and take action to avoid them. A leader may, for instance, set their phone to forward to voicemail during a time of day when they anticipate being readily distracted by phone calls.

Techniques for Recognizing Personal Distractions

Maintain a diary

You may learn more about your distractions by journaling your workday activities. Keep a record of what you were working on when you were sidetracked and why.

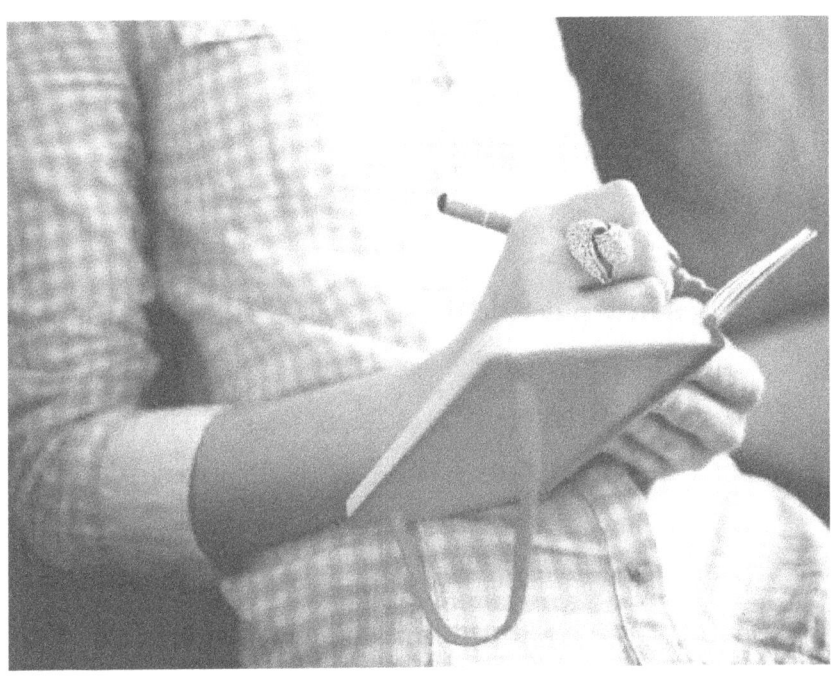

Make an analysis

Examine your record to look for any trends in the distractions you experienced. Do you, for instance, get sidetracked while working on a certain activity or at a certain time of day?

Ask for opinions

Ask your coworkers or family members what distracts you. They could provide you with a perspective you haven't thought about.

Explore various approaches

Attempt several distraction-reduction techniques. Consider working in a quiet place or using noise-canceling headphones if you are easily distracted by noise.

It is said that finding personal distractions is a crucial part of good time management for leaders. Successful leaders actively work to reduce or remove distractions because they know how they affect productivity. Leadership qualities include self-awareness, attention, time management, stress management, and proactivity. These traits enable individuals to recognize their distractions and take action to avoid them.

4.4 Strategies for avoiding distractions

Distractions may impede productivity and the advancement of objectives. As a leader, it's critical to recognize and deal with any distractions from our personal lives that can interfere with our job or the work of our colleagues. This section will look at various methods for avoiding interruptions and keeping your attention while working.

Knowing Your Distractions

Identifying distractions is the first step toward avoiding them. Typical personal distractions include the following:

- Technology: Distractions from work may be readily caused by checking emails, visiting social media, or utilizing other digital devices.
- Environmental distractions include chatty employees, disorganized offices, and uncomfortable seats.
- Personal Life: Stressors from home, including those related to family, health, or finances, might interfere with one's ability to focus at work.
- Disorganization: Disorganization may cause the time to be lost and deadlines to be missed.

Techniques for Reducing Distractions

After personal distractions have been recognized, there are several tactics that leaders may use to stay focused.

★ Time management may help leaders focus on high-priority projects by scheduling work and designating particular times for reading emails and other non-essential duties.

★ Eliminating Distractions: You can create a calmer and more concentrated workplace by removing physical distractions like mobile phones, turning off alerts, and wearing noise-canceling headphones.

★ Having specific goals and objectives may help leaders remain motivated and focused. These objectives must be time-bound, meaningful, quantifiable, and explicit (SMART).

★ Prioritizing Tasks: It's critical to order tasks according to their urgency and significance. Leaders will be better able to manage their time and stay organized.

★ Delegation: Productivity may be increased, and workloads can be decreased with effective delegation. Leaders should provide assignments to team members with the required knowledge and abilities.

★ Mindfulness practices: Deep breathing and meditation are two mindfulness practices that may help you focus and decrease stress.

★ Self-Care: Taking care of one's own needs may assist in enhancing overall well-being and lessen distractions. Such demands include getting adequate sleep, exercising, and eating healthily.

Examples of Distraction Prevention Techniques

Let's look at some instances when these tactics have been used successfully:

- ❖ Marketing manager John often needs to catch up on social media. He turns off alerts on his work gadgets and designates a certain daily period for monitoring his accounts.
- ❖ The project manager, Sarah, needs help concentrating in a loud workplace. To drown out irritating noises, she spends money on some noise-canceling headphones.
- ❖ CEO Mark needs to work on maintaining his attention on strategic goals because daily duties weigh him down. He assigns responsibilities to team members, freeing up his time to concentrate on the most important activities.
- ❖ Manager Jane often feels overburdened by her duties. Each day, she prioritizes her to-do list and allows her time appropriately, prioritizing urgent and significant things first.

Leaders often struggle with distractions but can control them by implementing good methods. Leaders may retain focus and accomplish their objectives by detecting personal distractions and putting into practice skills, including time management, reducing distractions, goal planning, prioritizing work, delegating mindfulness practices, and self-care.

Chapter 5: Decision-Making and Problem-Solving

Making decisions effectively is essential for every leadership role if the group or team is to succeed. Great leaders may be distinguished from ordinary ones by their capacity to make wise judgments. Consequently, it is crucial to grasp multiple decision-making frameworks to increase leadership effectiveness. The numerous decision-making models, their benefits and drawbacks, and the contexts in which they might be used are all covered in this chapter.

5. 1 Making informed decisions

The rational decision-making model is organized. It entails a sequential process of recognizing the issue, producing options, assessing the alternatives, choosing the best alternative, putting the choice into action, and tracking the outcomes. This model assumes that all relevant data is accessible and that the decision-maker is logical and impartial.

For Example: A business is thinking of introducing a new product. Doing market research, finding possible clients, analyzing the competition, assessing risks, and determining if the product is financially viable are all part of the decision-making process.

Benefits
The rational decision-making model offers a systematic process that guarantees all possibilities are considered and the optimal choice is based on the facts. The model makes the negative assumption that all information is accessible and that the decision-maker is unbiased and logical. Data could be lacking or inaccessible, and prejudices or emotions might sway the decision-maker.

Model for Intuitive Decision-Making
This model for making decisions based on intuition and judgment uses the decision-prior maker's experiences, intuition, and judgment. It includes making judgments quickly and based on experience without depending on in-depth study or research. A manager must

determine whether to employ a candidate based on their credentials, prior experience, and interactions with them during the interview.

Advantages: When time is important, the intuitive decision-making model may be helpful since it is rapid, effective, and depends on the decision-expertise maker and judgment.

Cons: Since the model is subjective, it may be swayed by prejudices, feelings, or unique ideas. The decision-maker could also fail to consider crucial facts or other possibilities.

Limited Reasoning Bounded rationality

It is a more practical decision-making method. It acknowledges that decision-makers need more time, information, or brainpower to absorb all the data. As a result, decision-makers often adopt heuristics or simplified decision rules. For instance, a manager must decide on a supplier for office supplies. They could depend on prior experiences or suggestions from peers rather than completing in-depth research on all possible providers.

Benefits: The bounded rationality model considers that decision-makers have a finite amount of time and money. It enables quick judgment using streamlined guidelines or heuristics.

The model could only consider crucial facts or other possibilities. The decision-maker could also depend on the information that is out-of-date or incorrect.

Model for Group Decision-Making

In the group decision-making model, a group collaborates to conclude. Usually, the procedure involves deliberation, consensus-building, and brainstorming. For example, a group chooses a project to work on. Before making a choice, the team members will debate several possibilities and assess the advantages and disadvantages of each option.

Benefits: The group decision-making paradigm enables a range of viewpoints and ideas to be considered, leading to a more well-informed choice. It also encourages collaboration and teamwork.

Cons: The approach may take a long time, leading to groupthink, in which people must weigh all their choices or alternatives properly.

In short, decision-making skills are essential for effective leaders. Leaders may make wise judgments by being aware of the many decision-making models and their benefits and drawbacks. Considering the facts at their disposal, the available time, and the objectives of their team or organization, leaders should choose the decision-making model that best suits the circumstances.

5.2 Gathering and analyzing information

Making wise judgments is one of the main duties of good leaders. They must be able to collect and evaluate data from various sources to achieve this. In this chapter, we will look at some of the methods and methods that efficient leaders use to obtain and evaluate data.

Information Gathering

Accurate and pertinent information must be gathered to make informed judgments. Successful leaders receive information from various sources, including internal and external reports, surveys, market research, and client feedback. They use their knowledge and intuition in addition to the facts.

Internal Reports: Internal reports may provide insightful information about the organization's performance. Effective executives use financial, sales, and performance reports to track the organization's development.

External Reports: External reports include information on the external environment in which the business works, including industry reports, competitor analysis reports, and economic studies. Effective leaders use these studies to spot trends, opportunities, and dangers.

Surveys: For obtaining data from clients, staff members, and other stakeholders, surveys are a helpful tool. Effective executives employ surveys to get input on the organization's culture, goods, and services.

Market research: Market research sheds light on consumers' requirements, tastes, and purchasing habits. Market research is a tool effective executives utilize to find new business possibilities and create new goods and services.

Customer Feedback: Consumer feedback may provide insightful information about the organization's assets and liabilities. Effective leaders utilize consumer feedback to enhance goods, services, and the customer experience.

Information Analysis: When information has been obtained, it is time to evaluate it to make wise judgments. Successful leaders use various information analysis methods, including SWOT, PEST, and cost-benefit analyses.

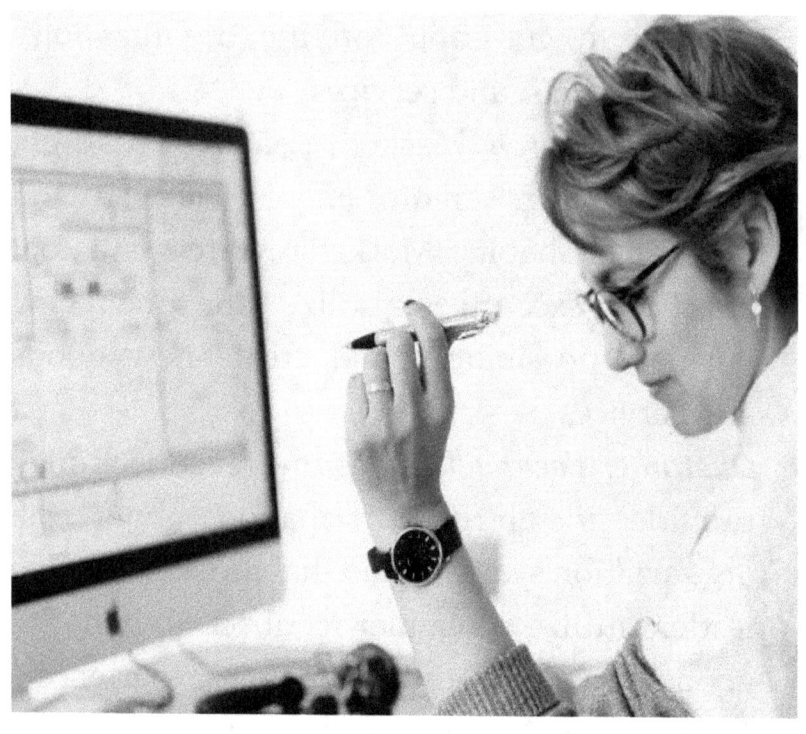

SWOT analysis is a strategic planning method that aids in determining an organization's strengths, weaknesses, opportunities, and threats. SWOT analysis is a tool used by effective leaders to create plans that take advantage of opportunities and strengths while addressing weaknesses and threats.

PEST Analysis: PEST analysis is a method for examining the organization's operating environment. Finding political, economic, social, and technical elements that influence the organization is helpful. PEST analysis is a tool used by effective leaders to spot patterns and foresee changes in the external environment.

Cost-Benefit Analysis: Cost-benefit analysis assesses the advantages and costs of a prospective course of action. Successful leaders evaluate a decision's financial viability and prospective risks and rewards using cost-benefit.

In conclusion, gathering and evaluating information is a crucial leadership ability. Leaders may take actions that advance the business by acquiring precise and pertinent data, interpreting it, and employing several strategies. Good leaders also know that making decisions is a continuous process that needs continuing oversight and modification as the external environment changes.

5.3 Identifying the problem

As a leader, you are often faced with finding solutions to challenging issues that need thorough consideration and judgment. Accurately defining the issue is one of the process's most important phases. By accurately defining the issue, you may create workable solutions beyond treating the symptoms to addressing the root causes.

This section will cover the significance of issue identification and practical problem-solving techniques.

Why Is It Necessary to Identify the Issue?

Accurately identifying the issue is essential because it frees you up to concentrate on developing solutions that tackle the problem's underlying causes. Without a thorough grasp of the issue, you risk coming up with remedies that deal with the signs and symptoms, which might cause additional difficulties and worse issues in the future.

Accurately diagnosing the issue may also help you save time, money, and resources. Knowing the underlying nature of the issue can help you avoid squandering money on ineffective remedies.

Techniques for Finding the Issue

Explain the issue at hand.

Start with defining the problem statement to find the issue. A well-defined problem statement should include details about the problem, its effects, the people involved, and the intended result. Also, it ought to be time-bound, relevant, explicit, quantifiable, and attainable (SMART). A SMART problem statement enables you to concentrate on the problem's most important components while avoiding side issues that might result in poor solutions.

The phrase "We are losing clients" is an example of a poorly articulated issue statement. What would be a SMART problem statement? "In the last year, our customer satisfaction ratings have dropped by 20%, which has cost us $1 million in sales. For the next six months, we must raise customer satisfaction scores by 10%."

Gathering information and data

You must acquire appropriate data and information to pinpoint the issue. Analyzing financial information, consumer and employee feedback, production data, and other pertinent sources may be part of this process. Analyzing the data, you may find trends, patterns, and probable issue sources.

For instance, you may collect information from customer care call records, feedback surveys, and complaints to uncover the cause of declining customer satisfaction ratings. You may use this information to determine consumers' most frequent problems, such as lengthy wait times or unhelpful customer support agents.

Do a root cause analysis

Finding the root causes of an issue is made easier with the use of the problem-solving approach known as root cause analysis. It entails continuously asking "why" to get at the source of the problem. You may create solutions that address the core problem rather than merely addressing the symptoms by determining the fundamental cause.

You may utilize root cause analysis to find why wait times are so long if you see that low customer satisfaction ratings result from lengthy waits. The problem is a shortage of employees or a poorly thought-out procedure. By addressing the fundamental reason, you may create practical solutions that decrease wait times and boost customer satisfaction.

List possible reasons for and remedies

You may collaborate with your team to find probable reasons and remedies after recognizing the issue and analyzing the root cause. No matter how outlandish they appear, encourage your employees to discuss their ideas. You could come up with novel solutions as a result of this that you had yet to think about previously.

For instance, if you have determined that lengthy wait times are the main factor contributing to declining customer satisfaction ratings, you might explore various remedies with your staff. This can include adding more personnel, streamlining the procedure, or implementing a self-service system that lets clients care for their requirements without waiting for a representative.

In summary, successful leadership involves a blend of many characteristics and abilities. Leaders may build a culture of trust and respect among their teams by continuously enhancing these skills and attributes, boosting output, job satisfaction, and overall performance.

5.4 Developing creative solutions and taking action

Several abilities and characteristics are necessary for effective leadership, including the capacity for problem-solving and idea generation via brainstorming. With the brainstorming approach, individuals or groups are encouraged to generate plenty of ideas quickly. This method might be particularly helpful for leaders who wish to promote an innovative and continuous development culture.

Traditional Brainstorming: In the classic brainstorming method, a group of individuals is gathered and asked to develop as many ideas as possible. This technique promotes free thinking and is often used to develop many ideas swiftly.

Mind Mapping: This brainstorming approach uses a visual diagram to express ideas and their relationships. This method is often used when arranging complex data or looking for connections between several concepts.

Reverse Brainstorming: Reverse brainstorming entails taking a fresh look at an issue. The question should be how to create the issue rather than how to fix it. This method might be helpful when attempting to identify possible barriers or impediments that could impede development.

Crawford's Slip Writing Technique: With this method, each team member is given a stack of index cards and instructed to jot down one idea on each card. The concepts may be arranged and categorized when all the cards have been gathered. The brainstorming approach known as "round robin" is traveling around the room and asking each team member to provide one idea at a time. This approach gives everyone an equal chance to participate and contribute their views.

Asking many questions in succession about a single concept or subject is known as starbursting. Who, What, When, Where, Why, and How may be queried. This approach promotes critical thinking and aids in the discovery of possible obstacles or possibilities. Successful leaders know that brainstorming can effectively develop ideas and find solutions. Using these several methods, leaders may foster innovation, cooperation, and creativity among their teams. Yet it's crucial to keep in mind that brainstorming is only one stage in the process of addressing problems. Before taking action, ideas need to be prioritized, polished, and subjected to analysis.

Evaluating options

Leaders must move quickly in today's fast-paced world and make choices that have a big effect on their teams and businesses. Leaders must be able to weigh choices and choose the best course of action since making good judgments is only sometimes simple. In this section, we will examine the characteristics and attributes of successful leaders, particularly their capacity for alternative analysis.

The Value of Options Analysis

A crucial part of the decision-making process is option evaluation. To make judgments that align with their business's objectives and core values, leaders must carefully consider all available possibilities. Leaders may make educated choices that reduce risks and maximize possibilities by weighing alternatives.

Several Methods of Options Evaluation

Successful leaders assess choices using a variety of methods. The following is a discussion of some of these methods:

Benefit-Cost Analysis

Determine the financial and non-financial costs and advantages linked to each choice using the cost-benefit analysis approach. Leaders may choose the option that offers the most advantages at the lowest cost by weighing the costs and benefits of each. For instance, a company owner could consider investing in new machinery for their facility. To ascertain the price of the equipment, the anticipated rise in productivity, and the return on investment, they would do a cost-benefit analysis. They would then evaluate which solution offers the most advantages by comparing this to the expense of maintaining the present equipment.

SWOT evaluation

SWOT analysis is a method for analyzing each option's strengths, weaknesses, opportunities, and threats. Leaders may choose the alternative that most closely reflects the objectives and tenets of their company by evaluating these variables. For instance, a business may be thinking of introducing a new product. To assess if introducing the product is the right course of action, they would do a SWOT analysis to identify its strengths and weaknesses, the market's opportunities and threats, and the competitors.

Analysis of Decision Matrices

A method for assessing choices based on a variety of factors is decision matrix analysis. Based on their company's objectives and guiding principles, leaders might give several criteria weights before comparing each choice to these weights. The greatest option is the one that receives the highest rating. For instance, a manager can be thinking about recruiting a new worker. Each applicant would be assessed based on credentials, experience, and cultural fit, with weights given to each factor per the company's objectives and guiding principles. The applicant with the highest score should be selected.

Pareto Analysis

The Pareto analysis approach may be used to identify the main causes of a problem or opportunity. By concentrating on the solutions that address the most important concerns, leaders may utilize this strategy to prioritize their choices. For instance, a manager can explore several strategies to lower staff turnover. They would do a Pareto analysis to determine the key causes of turnover, such as poor salaries or a lack of growth chances. They would then concentrate on choices that initially address these criteria.

Effective leaders need to have the essential ability of option evaluation. Leaders may make choices that align with their firm's objectives and values by employing tools like cost-benefit analysis, SWOT analysis, decision matrix analysis, and Pareto analysis. These methods aid decision-makers in objectively assessing possibilities, prioritizing them, and selecting the optimal course of action. By learning these approaches, leaders may enhance their decision-making abilities and help their companies succeed.

5.5 Implementing and evaluating solutions

In addition to problem-solving and decision-making, effective leaders must also be able to execute and assess solutions. A combination of strategic thought, good communication, and the capacity to carry out a plan of action is needed. The characteristics and attributes of successful leaders in implementing and evaluating solutions will be discussed in this chapter.

Step 1: Creating an Action Plan

Successful leaders are aware that the execution of any solution depends on a well-thought-out action plan. They develop a strategy outlining the measures required to accomplish their objectives in collaboration with their team. The strategy should include the timetables, benchmarks, and tools required for success. Successful leaders also ensure that team members, partners, and customers know the action plan clearly and understandably.

Example: The CEO of a tech firm has discovered a serious issue with the user interface of their website. Along with their development team, they produce a thorough action plan with predetermined benchmarks like wireframing, prototyping, and testing. The CEO also informs the marketing team of the strategy so that they are informed of any possible delays that would impact their promotional efforts.

Step 2: Implementation and Delegation
Effective leaders assign tasks and regularly monitor progress when the action plan is in place. They ensure everyone is aware of their obligations and tasks and provide help and

direction when necessary. They also have a backup plan in place if unforeseen problems occur.

Example: The building of a new office building is the responsibility of a construction company's project manager. They assign their team members jobs like supervising the interior, framing, and foundation construction. Also, the project manager keeps in constant contact with the client to provide updates on the project's development and resolve any issues that may come up.

Step 3: Assessment and Recommendations
Successful leaders know the significance of assessing the merits of their proposals. They routinely assess development and examine data to see if the solution performs as anticipated. They also welcome input from their staff and stakeholders to find areas for development and make the required modifications.

Example: A nonprofit group has launched a new initiative to combat homelessness in their town. The number of persons served, and their influence on their lives are only two examples of the program manager frequently gathering data to assess the program's performance. To pinpoint areas for development and modify the program as necessary, they also solicit input from the community, staff, and program participants.

Step 4: Ongoing Development
Successful leaders are always looking for ways to enhance their strategies and operations. They support their group's idea-sharing and creative problem-solving efforts. To ensure that their staff has the expertise and knowledge required to deliver successful solutions, they also prioritize professional growth and training.

For instance, a retail company's marketing manager is in charge of creating and executing fresh marketing strategies. They routinely engage in brainstorming exercises with their group to produce fresh concepts and spot areas for development. To make sure that their staff is knowledgeable on the most recent marketing trends and strategies, the marketing manager also offers training and development opportunities.

To conclude, successful leaders are adept at putting ideas into practice and assessing their success. They know the significance of creating an action plan, carrying out and assigning duties, assessing effectiveness, and constant development. Leaders may effectively implement and assess solutions to promote success in their company by embracing these characteristics and attributes.

Chapter 6: Leadership Styles and Strategies

There are many leadership styles and strategies that we will discuss in this chapter.

6.1 Understanding different leadership styles

Autocratic leadership

A leader who uses an autocratic leadership style makes judgements and gives orders without consulting or listening to their staff. A top-down management style and a hierarchical organizational structure are often linked to this kind of leadership. This chapter will examine the characteristics of autocratic leaders, their benefits and drawbacks, and the circumstances in which they may be effective.

Characteristics of Autocratic Leaders

One common perception of autocratic leaders is their authority, decisiveness, and control. They usually have a strong sense of direction and are extremely task-focused. The followings are some characteristics and attributes of authoritarian leaders:

- Authoritative: Autocratic leaders make all final decisions and have the last say in everything about their group or organization.
- Decisive: Autocratic leaders have a reputation for making choices quickly and without much involvement from others.
- Controlling: Autocratic executives often micromanage their employees because they have a strong desire for control.
- Task-focused: Autocratic leaders prioritize completing certain objectives and tasks above cultivating relationships with subordinates.
- Direct: Autocratic leaders often demand their followers to accept their orders without question and tend to communicate straightforwardly.

Autocratic Leadership's Benefits

Autocratic leadership has several benefits, which may make it useful in particular circumstances. These benefits consist of the following:

- Speed and Effectiveness: Decision-making may be quicker and more effective under autocratic leadership since no long discussions or disputes are required.
- Clear Expectations: Autocratic leaders set clear expectations for their employees, which may result in a more motivated and effective group.
- Consistency: Autocratic leaders often exhibit consistency in their decision-making and directive-giving, which may give their followers security and predictability.

Autocratic Leadership Drawbacks

Although autocratic rule may be efficient in certain circumstances, it also has some serious drawbacks. They consist of the following:

- Lack of Input: Autocratic executives often make choices without seeking input or feedback from their employees, which might prevent the team from being innovative and creative.

- Restricted Development: Autocratic leaders may need to allow their employees to advance their careers or take on new tasks, which may prevent the team from developing and growing.
- High Turnover: Subordinates under autocratic leadership may feel dissatisfied with their little input and control over their job, which may result in high turnover rates.

Circumstances in which autocratic rule is appropriate

Autocratic leadership may be suitable when efficiency and speed are essential, such as in a crisis or emergency scenario. It could also be suitable when the leader is the most competent to make choices due to their extensive knowledge and experience in the relevant field.

Steve Jobs, a co-founder and former CEO of Apple Inc., and Jack Welch, a former CEO of

General Electric, are two examples of autocratic CEOs. Both Jobs and Welch had a reputation for being decisive and in charge, which contributed significantly to the success of their respective businesses.

In certain circumstances, autocratic leadership may be successful, but it also has some serious disadvantages. Although autocratic leaders may be competent and efficient at attaining certain objectives, they don't allow their employees to advance their careers or take on new tasks. Before using an autocratic leadership style, leaders should evaluate the circumstances and weigh the possible benefits and drawbacks of doing so.

Democratic leadership

The success of every company depends on its leadership. Successful leaders need to make important choices and motivate and inspire their people to succeed. Democratic leadership, which strongly emphasizes participation and cooperation among team members, is one of the most successful leadership philosophies. We will examine the characteristics and attributes of successful leaders who use democratic leadership in this chapter.

Democratic leadership is a form of leadership in which the leader incorporates their team members in the decision-making process. This kind of leadership focuses on participation and cooperation, and the leader serves as a facilitator to help the team move towards its objectives. This kind of management may improve teamwork, morale, and job satisfaction.

Characteristics of Successful Leaders Who Adopt Democratic Leadership

Successful leaders that engage in democratic leadership have many characteristics that foster a collaborative and participatory atmosphere. Among these qualities are the following:

- Effective Communication: Team members are successfully communicated with by leaders who use democratic leadership. They build an atmosphere of openness and trust by actively listening, encouraging open communication, and doing so.
- Flexibility: Successful leaders who engage in democratic leadership are changeable. They urge their team members to think outside the box and are open to fresh perspectives.

- Leaders that use democratic leadership have emotional intelligence, enabling them to comprehend and control their own emotions and those of their team members. They can relate to their team members personally because they have empathy.
- The ability to solve difficulties is a trait of effective leaders who use democratic leadership. They urge their team members to recognize issues and work together to find solutions.
- Delegation: Team members are given duties and responsibilities by leaders who use democratic leadership. They have faith in the skills of their team members and give them the freedom to own their job.

Democratic leadership in Action Examples

Following are some instances of democratic leadership in different contexts:

The US Government: The US government is a prime illustration of democratic leadership.

The President is the leader, but they must collaborate with Congress and other government representatives to decide matters that have national implications. While making decisions, the President must take into account the suggestions and views of others.

Google: Google is renowned for its democratic management approach, encouraging staff members to express their ideas and thoughts. The creators of the business, Larry Page and Sergey Brin think that their success is a result of the creativity and invention of their staff.

Southwest Airlines: Another organization that employs democratic leadership is Southwest Airlines. Gary Kelly, the airline's CEO, is renowned for having an open-door policy and encouraging staff members to talk to him about their ideas and problems.

Democratic leadership provides several advantages, including the following:

Engagement and work satisfaction among employees rise when they are given a voice in decision-making because it makes them feel respected and appreciated, boosting both of these metrics.

- Better problem-solving: When team members communicate and exchange ideas, they can better recognize issues and discover solutions.
- Increased creativity and innovation: Team members' willingness to voice their thoughts and views may result in more imaginative and original solutions.
- Better retention rates: Workers are more inclined to remain with a firm when they feel appreciated and valued.

In short, democratic leadership, which promotes participation, cooperation, and open communication, is a successful leadership stance. Democratic leaders demonstrate characteristics such as good communication, adaptability, emotional intelligence, problem-solving abilities, and delegation. This leadership approach offers various advantages, including greater problem-solving, creativity and innovation, retention rates, and increased employee engagement and work satisfaction.

Laissez-faire leadership

Leadership is a crucial talent for a company to operate effectively. Successful leaders are renowned for their capacity to lead, inspire, and encourage their teams to succeed. There are many different leadership philosophies, each with pros and drawbacks. Laissez-faire leadership, commonly referred to as leadership, is one of the leadership philosophies. Under this leadership style, the team members are given the most latitude possible to decide what to do and how to accomplish it. The characteristics and attributes of good leaders will be discussed in this article, emphasizing the laissez-faire leadership style.

Laissez-faire leadership: what is it?

Under a laissez-faire leadership style, the team members get the bare minimum of direction from the leader and are free to decide what to do and how to do it. With this approach, the team's leader empowers the members to work freely while providing them with tools and assistance. The delegation leadership style is another name for the laissez-faire leadership style. The French expression "laissez-faire" (literally, "let it go") is the source of the English word "laissez-faire."

Characteristics and attributes of successful Laissez-faire leaders:

The following features and qualities characterize effective laissez-faire leaders:

- Successful Laissez-faire leaders have faith in their team members' capacity to come to choices and carry them out independently. They allow the team members to operate independently while providing the required tools and assistance. The connection between the team's leader and its members may be improved with the aid of this trust.

- Empowerment: A laissez-faire leadership approach allows team members to decide for themselves and accept responsibility for their job. When leaders employ this approach effectively, they provide their team members with the tools and support they need to feel empowered and motivated.
- Creativity: The laissez-faire leadership style promotes team members' imaginative problem-solving abilities. The team members may exercise their creativity to generate original ideas and solutions since they can choose and carry out their plans independently.
- Flexibility: Laissez-faire leaders that are effective are adaptive and flexible. They are receptive to new ideas and adjustments and provide the team members with the tools and assistance they need to make the adjustments.
- Effective leaders who use the laissez-faire leadership style must have excellent

communication skills. Communication becomes crucial to guarantee that everyone is on the same page since the leader offers little advice. To ensure that the team members understand their duties and responsibilities, great leaders adopting this approach communicate with them clearly and effectively.

Laissez-faire leadership examples

The founder of Virgin Group, Richard Branson, is renowned for his laissez-faire management style. He thinks allowing his workers the most freedom possible and letting them operate independently is important. He provides them with the tools and assistance they need but allows them the freedom to carry out their goals independently.

Steve Jobs was the co-founder of Apple Inc. and was well-known for his laissez-faire management style. He supported allowing his team members to decide for themselves and carry out their own ideas. He had faith in the people on his team's creative thinking and problem-solving skills.

The CEO of Berkshire Hathaway, Warren Buffett, is renowned for his laissez-faire management style. He gives his team members the tools and assistance they need, then allows them to operate independently. He supports giving the correct individuals autonomy over their job.

In conclusion, being a successful leader demands a variety of skills and abilities that are complicated and varied. Although some people are born with certain traits, others may acquire them through practice and concentrated effort. Effective leadership requires a variety of talents, many of which are discussed in this book, including active listening, nonverbal communication, cooperation abilities, decision-making, and time management.

Readers may learn more about what it takes to be a great leader and acquire the ability to guide others to success by thoroughly examining these issues. This book gives helpful advice and direction to help you develop your leadership skills and become a more successful and influential leader, whether you are an experienced leader trying to sharpen your abilities or a new leader just starting.

6.2 Learning to delegate and empower others

Each organization needs effective leaders to succeed, whether a small company, corporation, or government. The capacity to assign tasks and duties to team members is one of the fundamental abilities that all successful leaders need to have. The ability to delegate is a crucial one that not only helps team leaders manage their workload but also aids in the skill development of their team members. The many delegation techniques that good leaders use to make sure that their teams collaborate effectively and productively will be covered in this section.

Recognizing Delegation

Leaders provide tasks or make decisions to team members via delegation. It is essential to leadership since it enables team members to advance their careers and allows leaders to concentrate on their top objectives. The delegation, however, may be a difficult process that calls for leaders to have confidence in their team members, effective communication skills, and knowledge of each team member's strengths and shortcomings.

Delegation Techniques

Effective leaders use various delegation techniques to ensure that their teams are collaborating effectively and productively. Let's look at a few of the most popular delegation techniques below.

Choose the appropriate team member for the appropriate assignment.

While assigning duties, effective team leaders are aware of the team members' strengths and shortcomings. They understand that every team member brings different talents and experiences to the table that may be used to achieve certain tasks. To handle a difficult project, for instance, a team member with project management expertise may be more qualified than a team member with less experience.

Clarify your expectations.

Setting explicit expectations for what must be done, how it must be done, and when it must be finished is essential when assigning jobs. Good team leaders ensure everyone knows their responsibilities and provide them with the tools and encouragement they need to do the job.

Provide advice and assistance.
Effective leaders often give feedback and encouragement as their team members work on assigned tasks. This feedback may be coaching, constructive criticism, or praise, depending on the circumstance. Also, team leaders see that their members have access to the tools and assistance they need to do the job well.

Track development
Good leaders keep an eye on the progress of the tasks they have been given to ensure things are going as planned and spot any problems that should be fixed. Regular team meetings, project progress reviews, and performance

data analysis are all part of this process of finding development opportunities.

A follow-up

Effective leaders check in with team members after the assigned work is over to assess the results and give feedback on their performance. This aids team members in learning from their mistakes and developing their talents.

In short, all successful leaders need to be able to delegate effectively. It enables leaders to control their workload, enhance their team members' abilities, and ensure that their teams are collaborating effectively. Leaders may confidently assign work to their teams using the delegation techniques described in this book. By doing so, they will be ensuring their teams' success.

6.3 Empowerment techniques

Successful team leaders know that to achieve their organization's objectives, they must give their team members greater freedom to assume responsibility, make choices, and share their knowledge and abilities. Giving individuals the power, resources, and support they need to take responsibility for their job, make choices, and take action toward the common objective is empowerment. This chapter will examine the characteristics and skills that make a leader successful at inspiring and empowering their team.

Empowering team members may help a business in several ways, including boosting productivity, lowering turnover rates, and improving employee morale. Team members are more likely to be interested in their job and dedicated to attaining the organization's objectives when they feel appreciated and trusted.

Effective Leadership Characteristics for Empowerment
Successful team leaders have many characteristics, including:

→ Leaders who empower their team members must believe in their ability to make wise choices and accept responsibility for their job. They must also have faith in the abilities and knowledge of their team members to achieve success.

→ To empower team members, communication must be effective and clear. Expectations, objectives, and constructive criticism must all be communicated by leaders regularly.

→ Support: For their team members to be successful, leaders must provide them with the materials, equipment, and assistance they need. Offering coaching, mentoring, and training are all included in this.

→ Collaboration is necessary for empowerment because it enables team members and leaders to work together to accomplish common objectives. Leaders must be open to hearing the opinions and recommendations of their teams and incorporating those ideas into final decisions.

Effective leaders employ the following empowerment tactics to give their team members more control over their work:

- Assign work: Giving team members projects to complete boosts their confidence and enables them to learn new abilities. Effective leaders assign tasks based on the abilities and preferences of the team members.
- Leaders should provide development opportunities so that team members may gain new knowledge, take on more responsibility, and progress in their careers. Giving team members training and mentoring opportunities may help them learn new skills and boost their confidence.
- Promote innovation and creativity: Innovative and creative leaders give their teams the confidence to develop fresh concepts and methods. This may

result in enhanced procedures, goods, and services.

- Clarify your expectations: Clear expectations make it easier for team members to understand their roles and how their efforts support the company's objectives. Leaders must communicate clear expectations, and frequent feedback must be given.

Empowering techniques examples:
These are a few instances of excellent leaders inspiring their teams via the use of empowerment techniques:

Google: Google is renowned for its innovative and creative culture, where staff members are encouraged to think creatively and independently. The business allows staff members to work on side projects, which has resulted in the development of numerous popular products, including Gmail and Google Maps.

Starbucks: With training and development programs, Starbucks allows its workers to improve their careers. The business also provides workers with retirement plans, stock options, and extensive health benefits.

Zappos: Zappos has a distinctive strategy for handling customer service, allowing staff to choose what is best for the client. The organization provides its workers with training and assistance to ensure they have the abilities and information required to make these choices.

In conclusion, successful leadership requires empowerment as a key element. Leaders can develop a motivated and engaged staff dedicated to attaining common objectives by fostering trust, communication, support, and cooperation. Effective leaders may foster an empowering culture that benefits workers and the business by using strategies including job delegation, offering opportunities for advancement, fostering innovation, and establishing clear expectations.

6.4 Developing a Leadership Mission & Vision

For successful leadership, creating a mission statement is a crucial step. A mission statement describes a company's purpose, objectives, and values clearly and concisely. It helps to bring workers' actions and behaviors in line with the organization's broader vision by acting as a guiding principle for decision-making. The significance of a mission statement and how to create one will be discussed in this chapter.

Having a mission statement is important.

All companies, regardless of size, need a mission statement. It offers the following advantages:

★ Clarifies Purpose: An organization's mission statement explains its purpose in detail. It aids in the understanding of the company's mission and goals by stakeholders and workers.

★ Direction: A mission statement acts as a foundational premise for making decisions. It aids staff members in comprehending the steps they must take to accomplish the aims and objectives of the firm.

★ Employee Unification: A mission statement aids in bringing workers' activities and conducts into line with the company's overarching goals. It generates a culture focused on working as a team and building togetherness.

★ Builds Trust: A concise and unambiguous mission statement shows a company's dedication to its stakeholders, including clients, employees, and workers. It increases confidence and improves the company's reputation.

Creating a Mission Statement: The Process
Employees, stakeholders, and leaders work together to develop the mission statement. The procedures for creating a mission statement are as follows:

• Perform a SWOT analysis: A SWOT analysis must be done before creating a mission statement. The firm's strengths, weaknesses, opportunities, and dangers are all identified via this research.

- Determine Core Values: The next stage is to determine the business's core values. The company's core values are the guiding principles for achieving its objective. These principles must be consistent with the organization's overarching goals and vision.
- Define the Company's Purpose: The mission statement should clearly define the company's purpose. It should explain the existence of the firm.
- Outline the Company's Goals: The mission statement should describe the company's ambitions. These objectives must be time-bound, meaningful, quantifiable, and explicit (SMART).

After the procedures mentioned earlier are finished, it is time to develop the mission statement. The assertion must be concise, understandable, and clear. It should include the company's mission, guiding principles, and objectives.

The mission statement must be reviewed and improved as the last phase. To make sure that the statement truly represents the organization's mission, vision, and values, it should be evaluated by workers, stakeholders, and leaders.

Mission Statement Examples

Let's look at some mission statements from well-known businesses as examples:

- Tesla: To hasten the shift of the planet to renewable energy.
- Amazon: To be the world's most customer-focused business, allowing consumers to search for and learn about any product they would wish to purchase online.
- Nike's mission is to inspire and innovate for all athletes worldwide.
- Coca-Cola: To revive people's bodies, minds, and spirits.

- Google: Compile all available information into one easily accessible and practical place.

To conclude, being a successful leader requires developing a mission statement. It gives guidance, clarifies the point, unites the workforce, and fosters trust. A SWOT analysis, identifying fundamental values, defining the organization's purpose and objectives, writing the mission statement, and reviewing and revising the statement are all steps in creating a mission statement. A well-written mission statement is a basis for decision-making and aids in coordinating workers' activities and behaviors with the organization's overarching goals.

6.5 Leading with purpose

Creating a sense of purpose and meaning for the business and its members is crucial to effective leadership. It goes beyond just managing tasks and people. Leaders who can communicate and demonstrate their team's or organization's mission may inspire and drive their followers to reach higher levels of achievement. This chapter will discuss what it means to lead with purpose and how to cultivate it in yourself as a leader.

What is the point?

The reason something exists or is done is its purpose. The strategy, vision, and purpose of a company are all supported by this guiding concept. Our lives have meaning because of purpose, and organizations are no different. A shared sense of purpose gives an organization's members, from the executives to the frontline employees, a common direction and incentive. Without a defined mission, companies become aimless, unchanging, and uninspired.

Why is Leadership Purpose Important?

Purposeful leaders may motivate their employees to do great things. Leaders that are motivated by purpose may instill a feeling of direction and enthusiasm for the business's goals. They have the power to instill a feeling of trust, loyalty, and community among their followers. Even when faced with challenges and disappointments, purpose-driven leaders may aid their people in maintaining their attention on what matters most.

Leadership with Purpose: Advice and Techniques

Here are some pointers and techniques for leading with a purpose:

- Be Authentic: Sincerity is a must for purposeful leadership. You must support and uphold the organization's purpose and core principles. When you lead with sincerity, you will win your followers' respect and loyalty.
- Speak Clearly: You must express your intentions loudly and regularly if you want people to be inspired to follow your example. Use tales, anecdotes, and examples to make your idea real and concrete.
- Align Your Words and Your Actions: Your words and actions should be in line. It would help if you modeled the conduct

you wish to see in your followers. Make sure your activities, such as introducing green projects at your workplace, mirror your values, for instance, if your objective is to encourage sustainability.

- Encouraging Comments: Purposeful leadership is a collaborative effort. To ensure everyone is on board with your vision and objectives, invite comments and suggestions from your followers.
- Celebrate Your Successes: As You Go Along, Celebrate Your Successes and Milestones. Acknowledge and honor the achievements and efforts of your team. This will strengthen the feeling of motivation and purpose that underpins your team's work.

Leading with Action and Purpose

Steve Jobs is one example of a leader who personified the notion of leading with purpose. Jobs was renowned for his innovation-focused vision and ability to motivate his Apple team to produce products that profoundly impacted society. At Apple, Jobs had a clear vision: to build products that merged technology and design to improve people's lives. He held himself and his team responsible for carrying out this objective and passionately and firmly articulated this purpose. Apple was led by Jobs, who developed devices like the iPhone, iPad, and iPod that changed the computer sector and altered how people live and work.

Successful leadership is a broad and complicated issue requiring various abilities, attributes, and talents. Effective leadership requires a variety of talents, including the capacity to interact with others, manage time effectively, make wise judgments, and motivate followers to work towards a shared goal.

Chapter 7: Team Building and Collaboration

It is one of the essential skills to maximize your journey.

7.1 Building effective teams and fostering collaboration

Understanding group dynamics as a leader is essential to building a productive team. Group interactions, connections, and communication patterns are called group dynamics. We will examine the characteristics and attributes of successful leaders in this chapter to comprehend group dynamics.

Leaders must have a solid understanding of group dynamics to build a cohesive and successful team. Leaders can see possible problems and create plans to avoid them when they comprehend their team dynamics. They may also create an atmosphere at work that promotes effective communication and teamwork. Also, leaders may identify underperforming people and provide assistance to help them perform better by having a solid grasp of group dynamics.

Group dynamics & Influencing Factors

Several things may influence the dynamics of a group. These elements consist of the following:

- Group Size: Group dynamics may be significantly impacted by the group's size. Larger groups may be harder to control than smaller ones since the former tend to be more cohesive.
- Group objectives: The objectives of the group might affect group dynamics. The group will feel more united and collaborative if they work towards a

specific and shared objective. Yet, tension and disputes may arise if the group's objectives are ambiguous or in disagreement.

- Good communication is essential for maintaining positive group dynamics. Open and honest communication develops trust and encourages teamwork. Conversely, ineffective communication may result in misunderstandings, disputes, and anger.
- Roles and Responsibilities: The duties and responsibilities of each group member may impact the group dynamics. Understanding roles and duties among team members foster responsibility and cooperation. Roles and duties may be unclear, which can cause misunderstandings and disputes.

Group Dynamics Techniques

- Watch and Listen: Observing and listening to the group members is one of the best techniques for comprehending group dynamics. Leaders may learn more about the connections, interactions, and communication styles inside the group.

- Promote Honest and Open Communication: Group leaders should promote open and honest communication. They should provide a secure setting where participants may express their opinions without worrying about criticism or retaliation.
- Promote Trust: Effective group dynamics depend on developing trust within the group. Leaders can build trust by being open, keeping their word, and treating everyone with respect.
- Encourage Collaboration: Effective group dynamics depend on collaboration. Leaders should encourage members to collaborate, exchange ideas, and support one another.
- Handle Conflicts: Disagreements arise in every organization. Conflicts should be addressed head-on by leaders, who should also devise resolution plans. A breakdown in group dynamics and

animosity may result from ignoring problems.

Effective Group Dynamics Examples

Apple: Apple is a business renowned for having strong group dynamics. One of the most successful businesses in the world, the organization promotes a culture of innovation and teamwork.

Another organization with strong group dynamics is NASA. The organization's members feel united and cooperative because of the organization's clear and shared aim of space exploration.

The Beatles were a musical group that had strong group dynamics. Their willingness to cooperate and support one another was crucial to their success as they worked together to produce some of the most recognizable music in history.

To conclude, effective leadership requires a keen understanding of group dynamics. A cohesive and productive team that can accomplish its objectives may be built by leaders who are aware of group dynamics. They can recognize possible problems and create conflict prevention plans. They also encourage a climate of cooperation, confidence, and invention.

7.2 Building trust and respect

Creating a culture of trust and respect is essential to good leadership. Leaders who can establish strong bonds with their team members may foster a culture of trust and respect, which will enhance communication, boost engagement, and raise productivity. We will examine the characteristics and attributes of good leaders in this book as they develop respect and trust among their team members.

Establishing trust and respect in the workplace is crucial for many reasons. Team members are more inclined to be open and honest, to share their ideas, and to be responsive to criticism if they believe their leaders can be trusted. Better communication, more teamwork, and higher levels of involvement follow from this. Team members are more likely to be motivated, accept responsibility for their job, and be dedicated to attaining the team's objectives when they feel valued.

Characteristics of Successful Leaders in Fostering Respect and Trust

Successful leaders have a set of characteristics that enable them to foster a culture of respect and trust among their team members. A few of them are:

- Open Communication: Leaders who engage in open communication create trust with their team members by being forthright and sincere. They are friendly and promote open communication, which fosters a cooperative and respectful workplace.
- Active Listening: Leaders who give their team members their full attention show they appreciate their thoughts and viewpoints. As a result, the leader's team and themselves start to respect and trust them.
- Consistency: Team members appreciate and trust leaders who are constant in their words and deeds. Team members are more likely to feel confident in their leadership and follow it when they know what to anticipate from the team captain.
- Empathy: Leaders that exhibit empathy conveys to the team members that they are concerned about their welfare and are aware of their viewpoint. This encourages respect and trust and may raise spirits and increase involvement.

- Accountability: Team members are more likely to trust a leader who holds themselves responsible for their decisions. Leaders display their integrity and earn the respect of their team when they accept responsibility for their errors and aggressively try to rectify them.

Examples of Successful Leaders Developing Respect and Trust

Several successful leaders have promoted respect and trust among their staff. For instance, Microsoft CEO Satya Nadella is renowned for his compassionate leadership. He has received accolades for fostering a culture of respect and trust throughout the business, boosting creativity and teamwork.

Indra Nooyi, the former CEO of PepsiCo, is another example. Nooyi often had "skip-level" meetings with staff members as a sign of her dedication to fostering a culture of respect and trust in her organization. Throughout these discussions, she communicated directly with staff members at different organizational levels, displaying her openness and desire to listen.

In conclusion, successful leadership requires cultivating a culture of mutual respect and trust in a team. Building great connections with team members via open communication, active listening, consistency, empathy, and responsibility may boost engagement, productivity, and cooperation. We may improve our leadership abilities and create a more uplifting and successful work atmosphere by studying the characteristics and attributes of outstanding leaders in fostering trust and respect.

7.3 Understanding conflict and resolving conflicts

Conflict may happen everywhere; there are different perspectives, beliefs, or interests since conflict is an unavoidable element of human contact. Understanding the root causes of conflict and creating plans to handle it successfully are crucial leadership skills. The reasons for conflict in a leadership environment will be examined in this chapter, along with instances of how successful leaders may confront and resolve disagreements.

The Roots of War

Conflict may have many different root causes, but they can be generally divided into internal and external categories. Whereas external conflicts are brought on by other people, the environment, or events, internal conflicts originate inside the person. Successful leaders must be aware of the many sources of conflict and have the skills to see them in their teams. Some of the typical reasons for conflict are listed below:

- Communication problems: A communication breakdown is one of the most frequent reasons for conflict in every situation. Other prominent causes include misunderstandings and misinterpretations.
- Conflicts arising from differing values, ideas, and attitudes may occur when

persons with various personality types interact since personalities are all unique.

- Conflicts may arise when persons with different viewpoints, perspectives, or ways of thinking attempt to persuade others to perceive things by their way of thinking.
- Restricted resources: When individuals vie for access to scarce resources like time, money, or materials, conflict may result.
- Conflicts may result from power imbalances when individuals strive to increase their influence or make their authority known.
- Organizational change: When employees become used to new jobs, responsibilities, and working methods, organizational changes may lead to conflict.

Conflict Resolution

Successful leaders are adept at handling conflict because they recognize its inevitability. They use their communication and negotiating abilities to resolve disputes and maintain wholesome working relationships within their teams. Effective leaders use the following techniques to handle conflict:

- ❖ Successful leaders show empathy and understanding by actively listening to the opinions and concerns of their team members.
- ❖ Setting clear boundaries and expectations helps prevent misunderstandings and misinterpretations that may result in conflict.
- ❖ Collaboration is encouraged because it fosters a culture of trust and respect among team members, which lessens the risk of confrontations.
- ❖ Leaders may mediate, bringing disparate groups together to devise a compromise to end a problem.
- ❖ Conflict resolution education: Leaders may invest in conflict resolution education for their teams to help them

recognize and successfully handle disagreements.

❖ Successful leaders put their attention on shared beliefs and objectives rather than allowing disputes to arise from differences.

Examples

Effective leaders may use several approaches to handle and end disagreements. These are some instances of how managers have handled disputes in their teams successfully:

- By listening actively, a team leader identified a dispute between two team members over differing viewpoints. The team's leader attentively listened to both members, grasping their viewpoints and identifying points of agreement. The disagreement was settled, and the team members could now function as a unit.
- Promoting cooperation: A team leader discovered disagreements due to team members vying for limited resources. The team's leader promoted cooperation

and teamwork, assisting team members in cooperating more efficiently to distribute resources.

- Mediation: A team leader saw a personality problem between two team members. As a mediator, the team's leader brought the two parties together to establish an agreement. The team's ability to collaborate successfully led to an improvement in the team's working relationship.
- Goal-setting, time management, decision-making, problem-solving, communication, delegating, empowerment, and group dynamics are characteristics and skills that good leaders must possess. To accomplish their objectives, guide their teams, and have a good effect on their businesses and society, successful leaders have these qualities and are always working to improve them.

Each of these characteristics and talents was thoroughly examined in this book, offering readers useful advice, suggestions, and case studies for improving their leadership abilities. From understanding the varied leadership types to creating trust and respect across teams, this book addresses the important characteristics of successful leadership that can be utilized in any environment.

7.4 Conflict resolution techniques

Each workplace will inevitably see conflict. Thus good leaders must be able to handle it. Divergent viewpoints, personality conflicts, and conflicting interests are only a few examples of the many potential drivers of conflict. Controlling may result in improved production, morale, and possibly legal action. Effective leaders may, however, use various strategies to settle disputes productively and advantageously. This book will examine some of the best methods for managing disagreements and fostering positive working relationships among leaders.

Understanding the origins of conflict: Before conflict resolution, it is important to comprehend the causes of conflict. Disputes may result from a variety of factors, such as:

- personality variations
- Miscommunications or misunderstandings
- different aims or goals
- contrasting morals or views
- limited resources or resource competition
- Organizational restructuring or change

To successfully settle conflicts, leaders must be able to pinpoint their root causes. This calls for attentive listening, empathy, and comprehension of each party's viewpoint.

Efficient methods for resolving disputes

- ❖ Cooperation entails bringing all sides to a disagreement together to achieve a shared resolution. This method promotes candid conversation, original problem-solving, and understanding between parties. When both sides are dedicated to working together and are prepared to make concessions to achieve a mutually beneficial agreement, collaborative conflict resolution is successful.

❖ Finding a middle ground where both sides may agree to give up something to achieve a settlement is known as a compromise. This method calls for strong negotiating and communication skills and an openness to hearing and comprehending other people's viewpoints.

❖ To overcome the issue, accommodation is the act of one side caving into the other party's demands. This tactic is helpful when the problem is small, or the parties' connection is more significant than the actual issue.

❖ Avoidance: Avoiding the disagreement briefly gives the emotions a chance to settle. This strategy might be useful when the situation is not urgent, and the parties can have a more reasoned debate after some time.

❖ Competition: In a dispute, one side often prevails, and the other loses. Only employ this method if there is no other choice and the situation is urgent. When maintaining a pleasant connection between parties is crucial, competition should be avoided.

Conflict resolution strategies examples
- Collaboration: When two team members disagree on a project's best course of action, the team leader may cooperate to settle the issue. The team leader could convene the two sides to come to a compromise that considers their viewpoints.
- Compromise: A manager may compromise to settle a dispute between two workers whose work schedules are incompatible. The manager may collaborate with the staff to develop a timetable that suits everyone.
- Accommodation: An HR manager may utilize accommodation to settle a dispute between workers and their management.

The employee could agree to take on extra tasks to assist the boss in achieving their goals.

- Avoidance: A team leader may utilize avoidance to settle a dispute between two team members with contrasting personalities. The team leader could suggest that the two sides separate from one another so they can return to the situation with new eyes.
- Competition: A CEO may utilize competition to settle a dispute between two departments vying for the same resources. The CEO may distribute resources according to performance criteria, with the best-performing department getting the required funding.

Effective leadership is crucial to the success of any organization or group in light of the above. It necessitates a mix of abilities that can be cultivated and perfected through time. This book examines several facets of successful leadership, such as time management, decision-making, delegating, and dispute resolution.

7.5 Encouraging diversity and inclusivity in teams

Diversity is more crucial than ever in modern society. Globalization makes us live in a much more linked and reliant society. As a leader, it is crucial to comprehend the problems and possibilities of a diverse team since diversity has its challenges. In this chapter, we'll look at the characteristics and skills that make for good leaders who also understand diversity.

Understanding Diversity

A thorough understanding of diversity is the first step to being a successful leader in a varied setting. Beyond race and ethnicity, diversity includes gender, age, religion, culture, language, financial position, and other factors. Successful team leaders know that diversity is more than simply tolerance; it's also about valuing the distinctions that make each team member special. Leaders may create an atmosphere where all team members feel appreciated and respected by fostering a culture that embraces diversity.

Creating a Diverse Team

It's critical to create a team that accurately represents the variety of the organization's stakeholders to manage a varied team successfully. This entails aggressively bringing on board and keeping team members from various backgrounds. But, it's crucial to foster a climate where all team members feel appreciated and involved instead of just hiring a diverse staff. To do this, the team must make a deliberate effort to identify and resolve any prejudices or discrimination that could present.

Effective Communication

In every leadership position, effective communication is crucial but crucial in a varied team context. It's crucial to be aware of these distinctions and modify your communication style appropriately since various cultures and backgrounds may have different communication styles. Leaders must also ensure that every team member feels free to voice their views regardless of background. Building an environment of trust and respect may be facilitated by encouraging open conversation and active listening.

Handling Bias and Discrimination
Bias and prejudice may still exist even in environments that are made to be inclusive. Successful leaders must be equipped to deal with these problems quickly and successfully. This necessitates a readiness to hear concerns and respond appropriately. Also, it entails educating the group about the value of diversity and the negative consequences of prejudice. Leaders may develop a culture of respect and inclusiveness by confronting prejudice and discrimination head-on.

Successful leaders are aware of the value of continuing training and development for the members of their teams. This is particularly crucial in a varied team setting because team members may have various educational backgrounds and skill levels. Giving team members a chance for training and development may help guarantee that everyone has the resources necessary for success in their positions. It also assists team members in comprehending the value of diversity and acquiring the abilities necessary to function well in a varied team setting.

A knowledge of diversity, effective communication, confronting prejudice and discrimination, and continual training and growth are all necessary for successful leadership in a varied setting. Leaders may ensure that all team members feel appreciated and have access to the resources they need to succeed by fostering respect and inclusiveness. Leaders may guide their teams to success in a multicultural and globalized environment by having the necessary talents and attributes.

7.6 Encouraging inclusivity

Effective leaders must foster an inclusive atmosphere where everyone feels appreciated and respected in today's varied and multicultural companies. An important leadership quality that may assist businesses in creating a supportive and effective work environment is encouraging inclusion. This chapter will discuss the value of inclusion in leadership and provide tips for managers on promoting and maintaining inclusivity at work.

The value of inclusion in leadership: Diversity comes in many forms, including color, ethnicity, gender, age, religion, sexual orientation, etc. Being inclusive involves respecting diversity in all of its manifestations. It is a crucial leadership quality because it fosters a feeling of community, fosters invention and creativity, and boosts morale and productivity. Encouragement of inclusion by leaders increases the likelihood that varied talent will be attracted and retained, which may result in a better knowledge of audiences, markets, and communities.

Ways to promote diversity
Support open communication: Provide a secure environment where staff members may

voice their thoughts and ideas without worrying about being judged or criticized. This may be accomplished by conducting regular team meetings, setting up channels for employee input, and giving staff members frequent opportunities to voice their opinions.

- ❖ You may celebrate diversity by honoring many cultural and religious holidays and commemorations. This may be accomplished by planning cultural events, encouraging staff members to share their experiences and tales, and offering opportunities for growth and learning.
- ❖ Employee knowledge and comprehension of diversity and inclusion will improve with the help of training and education. Workshops, seminars, and online courses can help with this. Employees may improve their intercultural competency via training, which can also increase their ability for empathy and understanding.

❖ Recognize your unconscious prejudice and take action to correct it. Leaders must be aware of their own unconscious biases. This may be done through developing rules and procedures to reduce prejudice, offering diversity and inclusion training, and cultivating an open and conscious workplace culture.

❖ Encourage workers to express their viewpoints and ideas by forming cross-functional teams and fostering cooperation. By doing so, silos may be broken down, creating an inclusive work atmosphere.

❖ Lead by example: Leaders must set an example for others to follow and show that they value diversity, equality, and justice in all facets of the workplace. Establishing rules and procedures that encourage inclusion, encouraging gender and cultural diversity in hiring, and building a diverse leadership team are all ways to do this.

Leadership that is inclusive examples

CEO of Microsoft Satya Nadella: At Microsoft, Satya Nadella has promoted diversity and inclusiveness by implementing various programs to benefit women and underrepresented groups. Microsoft has established an inclusive culture that values individuality and encourages equal opportunity for all workers under his direction.

CEO of Starbucks Kevin Johnson: At Starbucks, Kevin Johnson has elevated diversity and inclusion to a primary focus. He has put in place various efforts to advance diversity, such as mentoring programs, unconscious bias training for staff, and diverse recruiting procedures. Starbucks has also created a Diversity, Equality, and Inclusion Council to guide the organization's efforts.

John Donahoe, the CEO of Nike, has made inclusion a fundamental principle of the company and has put various programs in place to support diversity and equality. They include funding initiatives that assist underrepresented groups, encouraging diverse leadership, and putting in place regulations to ensure equitable pay and employment opportunities for all workers.

In conclusion, inclusiveness is an important leadership quality that may assist firms in creating a supportive and effective workplace. Successful leaders must foster an atmosphere where everyone is treated with respect and worth. Through fostering open dialogue, recognizing diversity, offering instruction and training, being conscious of unconscious prejudice, and fostering varied viewpoints

Chapter 8: Ethics and Social Responsibility

Making ethical judgments is a skill that is necessary for effective leadership, in addition to decision-making abilities. Ethical decision-making models provide an organized method to ensure that ethical issues are taken into account throughout the decision-making process. In this chapter, we will look at many ethical decision-making models and how they apply to leadership.

8.1 Knowing How to Make Ethical Decisions

To make morally sound decisions, one must consider moral principles like justice, fairness, and respect for others. While making choices, effective leaders must strike a balance between their values and views and ethical issues. A framework for examining moral quandaries and choosing a course of action that complies with ethical standards is provided by ethical decision-making models.

Models for Ethical Decision-Making:
There are several ethical decision-making frameworks, each with a method for examining ethical conundrums. Among the most popular models are:

- The practical approach prioritizes the overall good or benefits for the largest possible population. It entails analyzing the advantages and disadvantages of each option to choose the one that will benefit the most people overall.

- An executive of a firm may have to decide whether to fire employees to save expenses. To evaluate which course of action would result in the greatest good for the most people, the practical method would include considering the advantages and disadvantages of each possibility.
- The rights approach places a strong emphasis on upholding people's inalienable rights. It entails assessing which action will most effectively uphold the rights in the judgment and

recognizing the rights at stake. Example: A healthcare organization's executive may need to decide whether to provide patient information. The rights method entails considering which course of action will best uphold the basic rights in the choice, such as the patient's right to privacy.

- The Justice Approach: This strategy guarantees equality and justice in decision-making. It entails identifying the relevant stakeholders and determining what is reasonable and fair for each. For instance, a government agency manager could have to decide how to allocate resources. The justice method would include identifying the relevant parties, such as various populations or regions, and determining what would be right and fair regarding resource distribution.

- The virtue approach strongly emphasizes one's character and the characteristics required for making moral choices. Finding the qualities required for making ethical decisions and incorporating them into the decision-making process are both involved.

- A charity organization's leader could decide whether to accept a gift from a business with a dubious reputation. Under the virtue approach, the decision-making process would be guided by qualities essential for moral decision-making, such as honesty and integrity.

Application of Ethical Decision-Making Models in Leadership

To make morally sound decisions, leaders must be able to use ethical decision-making models. This entails recognizing ethical problems, examining the circumstance using an ethical decision-making model, and deciding on an ethically sound plan of action.

For instance, a manager at a financial institution could have to decide whether to grant a loan to a client who doesn't fulfill the credit requirements. The decision-maker might use the practical method to compare the advantages and disadvantages of each option, such as whether to approve the loan and boost the institution's earnings or refuse the credit and possibly put the client in financial difficulties. The decision-maker also utilizes the rights-based perspective to pinpoint the basic rights at stake, including the customer's right to fair treatment, and then decide which course of action would most effectively uphold those rights.

In light of the above, effective leadership is crucial to organizational success. With this section, we have examined the characteristics and skills of good leaders and the methods and approaches they may use to make wise choices, resolve disputes, foster a climate of trust and respect, and advance diversity and inclusivity at work.

Leadership is more than simply making choices and assigning duties; it's also about getting to know people, cooperating with them, fostering a great workplace culture, and supporting moral principles. For their team to succeed, effective leaders must be able to inspire and encourage everyone on the team. They combine a variety of abilities, including delegation, problem-solving, communication, and decision-making, and they are always changing and adjusting to new situations.

8.2 The role of values in decision-making

A strong sense of values and a commitment to make choices that are consistent with those values are necessary for effective leadership. This chapter will discuss the relevance of values in decision-making and how strong leaders utilize their values to inform their decisions. We will look at how values influence decisions, how values affect corporate culture, and how leaders can foster a values-driven workplace.

Decision-Making and Values: Values serve as the guiding principles that both people and organizations use to decide what to do and how to do it. They stand for our core values, what we stand for, and what we believe in. Our values are a compass for making difficult choices because they influence our beliefs, attitudes, and actions.

Values are crucial in the context of leadership while making decisions. Successful leaders know that their actions reflect their beliefs and must be consistent with the organization's ideals. CEOs who put their beliefs above those of the company risk running afoul of their team and the overall corporate culture.

The Effect of Values on Organizational Culture

An organization's culture is shaped by its leaders' values, which affect workers' behavior. If executives emphasize moral conduct, truthfulness, and integrity, the organization's culture is likely to reflect these ideals. On the other hand, the culture will also be represented if leaders prioritize profit at any cost or their interests above the firms.

A good and effective work environment is produced by leaders who prioritize values that coincide with those of the business. This kind of work atmosphere encourages innovation, cooperation, and the sharing of ideas and draws workers with similar beliefs.

Creating a Values-Driven Workplace

Leaders may create a values-driven workplace by setting an example for others to follow. Leaders create an atmosphere where these values are reinforced and promoted by exhibiting a dedication to moral conduct, honesty, and integrity.

Also, executives can consistently and effectively convey the organization's principles. Mission statements, corporate principles, and frequent staff communication are effective ways to do this. Building trust with their team and reiterating the significance of the organization's principles are two things leaders who communicate those values transparently and genuinely do.

Also, managers may promote employee input and utilize it to help them make choices consistent with the company's values. Leaders may foster a feeling of ownership and buy-in that can enhance engagement and productivity by including staff in decision-making and appreciating their contribution.

Examples of leadership that is values-driven:
In the corporate sector, there are many instances of values-driven leadership. Patagonia, a clothing brand renowned for its dedication to sustainability, has always put the environment's well-being ahead of its bottom line. The firm is dedicated to "using business to inspire and execute solutions to the environmental issue," according to its mission statement.

Similarly to this, Starbucks has made principles like inclusiveness and diversity a priority. Starbucks CEO Kevin Johnson said the firm encourages "inclusion, diversity, and equality for all individuals." The corporation has implemented various programs to advance these ideals, such as training on unconscious bias and assistance with employee-run affinity clubs.

In conclusion, effective leadership requires having strong values. Top talent is attracted to and retained by leaders who prioritize values consistent with the organization's ideals. Leaders may foster a values-driven workplace based on trust and respect by demonstrating the conduct they want to see in others, conveying the organization's values clearly and consistently, and including workers in the decision-making process.

8.3 Developing a sense of social responsibility and empathy

Social responsibility is a crucial component of every firm or person in modern society. Each has an ethical duty to the society they live in, which is known as social responsibility. It is about giving back to society and helping to improve the neighborhood. Successful leaders know the value of social responsibility and work to improve society. This chapter examines how ethical leaders integrate social responsibility into their decision-making and its leadership role.

What Is Social Responsibility?

Social responsibility is the moral duty that all people and organizations have to behave in ways that benefit society. It involves thinking about how our behaviors affect society and taking action to reduce detrimental effects while enhancing beneficial effects. Environmental responsibility, community participation, and corporate moral conduct are all examples of social responsibility.

The importance of social responsibility in leadership

Successful leaders are aware of their obligation to the society in which they work. They are conscious of the potential effects of their activities on the neighborhood and strive to have a good influence. Effective leadership requires social responsibility because it enables leaders to build a favorable reputation for themselves and their businesses. Moreover, it aids in establishing credibility and trust with stakeholders, including clients, workers, and investors.

Considering social responsibility while making decisions

Effective leaders integrate social responsibility into their decision-making processes by considering how their choices will affect society. They take action to prevent negative effects while increasing favorable effects because they know their actions have repercussions. To reduce its harmful environmental effects, a corporation could employ eco-friendly materials in its goods. Another example is when a business gives back to the community by donating a percentage of its earnings to a nonprofit organization.

Applying Social Responsibility at Work

Good leaders know that social responsibility extends beyond giving to charities or volunteering at events for the community. It also involves putting in place moral business principles that benefit society. This entails fostering a diverse and welcoming workplace, encouraging ethical hiring procedures, and reducing the damaging effects of their activities on the environment.

Businesses that have integrated social responsibility into their operations include many instances of socially responsible businesses. For instance, the clothing firm Patagonia is dedicated to utilizing eco-friendly materials in its goods and supporting ethical labor methods. Another example is the ice cream maker Ben & Jerry's, dedicated to utilizing non-GMO products and promoting fair trade principles.

In summary, social responsibility is a crucial component of good leadership. Successful leaders are aware of their obligation to the society in which they operate and work to have a good influence. They employ ethical business practices that benefit society and integrate social responsibility into their decision-making processes. Companies that practice social responsibility get respect from stakeholders and gain their confidence and credibility. Leaders must, therefore, recognize the importance of social responsibility and work to benefit society.

8.4 Making ethical decisions and taking responsibility

Various skills and attributes are necessary for effective leadership, enabling leaders to manage their teams or organizations successfully. Taking responsibility for one's actions is a key quality of successful leaders. Individually accountable leaders establish an example for their teams, encourage accountability, and foster trust and confidence in their followers. We will discuss the value of personal accountability in successful leadership in this chapter and how leaders may cultivate and exhibit this quality.

Definition of Personal Responsibility

The notion that each person is in charge of their own choices, actions, and results is called personal responsibility. Personal responsibility in leadership refers to a leader's ownership of their choices, acceptance of the repercussions of their decisions, and accountability for the success of their group or organization.

Proactive, self-driven, and responsible are all aspects of personal responsibility, and they help leaders gain the respect and trust of their team members.

Personal responsibility is an important quality for successful leadership. Hence it is important in the field of leadership. Individual accountability for one's actions and choices is encouraged across the company by leaders who set a good example for their team members. Since they are seen as dependable, dependable, and trustworthy, leaders who exhibit personal accountability are likely to inspire trust and confidence in their team members.

Leaders may promote a culture of continuous improvement by encouraging personal responsibility, accountability, and trust. Leaders may see opportunities for improvement and take the initiative to solve them by taking responsibility for their actions and results. This might encourage development inside the company and stimulate innovation.

Personal Accountability
A crucial component of successful leadership is the development of personal accountability. Here are several methods for leaders to cultivate and display this quality:

- Establish Clear Expectations: Team leaders should ensure that all team members know their roles and duties and are clear about what is expected of them. Leaders may encourage their teams to take responsibility for their work and results by establishing clear expectations.
- Promote Accountability: Leaders should encourage accountability across the board and hold themselves and their teams accountable for achieving their targets. Leaders may motivate their team members to take ownership of their actions and choices by setting a good

example and keeping themselves responsible.

- Accept Failure: Instead of seeing failure as a setback, leaders should see it as a chance for development and learning. Leaders may show personal accountability and motivate their team to follow suit by accepting failure and owning their errors.
- Actively solicit team member input. Leaders should also be receptive to constructive criticism. Leaders may show personal accountability and promote a culture of continuous development by listening to criticism and acting to address areas for improvement.

Examples of leadership with personal responsibility

These are a few instances of leaders that exhibit personal accountability:

- Satya Nadella, Microsoft's CEO: Nadella has adopted a growth mentality and encouraged a culture of innovation and constant learning as his contribution to the company's success.

- General Motors CEO Mary Barra: By making adjustments to enhance safety and quality and by leading by example for her staff, Barra has accepted responsibility for the business's prior shortcomings.
- Former Starbucks CEO Howard Schultz showed personal accountability by accepting responsibility for the company's errors and taking corrective measures, such as adopting a more inclusive and diverse employment policy.

Personal accountability is an essential quality for successful leadership. Ownership of one's actions and choices sets a good example for others on one's team, encourages responsibility, and fosters trust and confidence. Leaders may create a culture of continuous improvement and promote success in their businesses by practicing and modeling personal responsibility.

8.5 Being accountable

A crucial quality of successful leaders is accountability. Leaders must be accountable for their actions and choices if they want to help their teams and organizations accomplish their objectives. Leaders gain the respect, credibility, and confidence of their team members, clients, and stakeholders when they accept responsibility for their actions. In this book, we will discuss the significance of accountability, how it connects to leadership, and how to foster responsibility in both yourself and your team.

Why Leadership Accountability Is Vital

Since it encourages trust, openness, and responsibility, accountability is a crucial component of good leadership. Leaders who take responsibility for their actions demonstrate dedication to their group, organization, and objectives. They exhibit honesty, a quality that is essential for good leadership. The following are some arguments in favor of accountability in leadership:

- Creates trust: Leaders establish trust with their teams when they take responsibility for their actions. When team members know their leader is prepared to accept responsibility for their actions, they have greater faith in their choices.
- Responsibility is demonstrated: Accountable leaders show that they are in charge of the success of their group. They are willing to accept responsibility for the choices and actions made by their team.
- Promotes openness: Accountable team leaders promote openness among their members. They are willing to be truthful and open about their choices and actions, which promotes a culture of openness throughout the company.
- Enhances performance: Leaders are more likely to perform well when held responsible for their decisions. They lead

by example, inspiring their team members to accept accountability for their actions and raise the bar on their work.

Ways to Hold Your Leaders Responsible
It can improve your ability to be responsible over time. It requires a dedication to integrity, accountability, and openness. These are a few methods for leaders to take responsibility:

- Be accountable for your actions: Leaders must be accountable for their choices, decisions, and errors. This entails being prepared to acknowledge your errors and act to remedy the problem.

- Clear communication is essential between team members and leaders. Setting clear expectations, giving input, and receiving feedback from others are all part of this.
- Establish objectives: Team leaders should establish specific objectives for themselves and their teammates. This promotes an accountability culture inside the company.
- Tracking progress will help leaders keep themselves and their team members responsible for reaching their objectives.
- Leadership requires transparency, both in terms of choices and deeds. This entails being forthright and sincere about your actions and motivations.

Instances of Leadership Accountability

There are several instances of leaders who have shown their responsibility through their deeds and choices. To name a few:

- Alan Mulally: Ford was experiencing financial difficulties when Alan Mulally took over as the company's CEO in 2006. Mulally was in charge of turning the business around, and he accomplished this by carrying out a thorough reorganization plan that called for shutting down plants and reducing expenses. Mulally was open and honest about the issue, and he told his team members exactly what had to be done to salvage the business.
- Mary Barra: General Motors was in a crisis due to defective ignition switches that had resulted in several fatalities when Mary Barra was appointed CEO of the business in 2014. Barra swiftly resolved the situation since she was responsible for the company's conduct. She established a fund to repay victims and their families and put new safety measures in place to stop incidents from happening again.

- Jeff Bezos: Jeff Bezos is a well-known American business tycoon, philanthropist, and entrepreneur. He is regarded as one of the most important individuals in the world and the creator of Amazon, the biggest online retailer in the world. Bezos was raised in Houston, Texas, after being born in 1964 in Albuquerque, New Mexico. He earned electrical engineering and computer science degrees from Princeton University.
- Bezos established Amazon.com in his garage in 1994, and it has since expanded to rank among the world's biggest and most prosperous online retailers. Bezos led Amazon as CEO until July 2021, when he resigned to take on the role of executive chairman of the board. He expanded Amazon's operations into a wide variety of sectors, from cloud computing to grocery delivery, during his tenure as CEO, turning the company into a digital behemoth.

- Bezos is renowned for his creative and progressive leadership style, often taking chances and acting boldly to keep one step ahead of the competition. He famously said, "We're not competitor-focused, we're customer-focused," demonstrating his sincere support for customer-centric company strategies.

In addition to his commercial endeavors, Bezos is dedicated to charity and contributing to society. He established the $2 billion Day One Fund in 2018 to help homeless families and build a network of preschools in neglected areas. Bezos has also donated millions of dollars to scientific research and exploration through his private spaceflight company, Blue Origin.

Jeff Bezos is an intriguing person who exhibits many characteristics and virtues of successful leaders. His visionary approach to business, commitment to innovation, and dedication to positively impacting society make him a valuable case study for anyone interested in exploring leadership and entrepreneurship.

Chapter 9: Applying Leadership Skills in the Real World

In this chapter, we will learn to apply leadership skills in the real world.

9.1 Applying leadership skills in community

No one position or title may claim to be a leader. It is a trait that everybody may exhibit in any situation, whether personal or professional. A leader must see opportunities where they may use their knowledge and talents to make a difference and have a clear grasp of their strengths and shortcomings. The characteristics and attributes of successful leaders in spotting leadership opportunities will be discussed in this chapter.

Characteristics and Skills of Successful Leaders

Visionary

Visionaries with a solid grasp of their goals and objectives are effective leaders. They take a proactive stance and always look for chances that fit their vision. They can also communicate their vision to others and motivate them to work together to realize the shared objective.

Threat Taker

Effective leaders are okay with taking measured risks. They are aware that success and development can require taking risks. They are open to new experiences and self-assured in their capacity to succeed.

Adaptable

Successful leaders may evolve with the times. They can modify their plans and methods as necessary to remain on course and accomplish their objectives. They also recognize that change is inevitable and may bring new opportunities for development and creativity.

Resourceful

Resourceful and capable of coming up with original answers to issues, effective leaders. They can use their network and resources to accomplish their goals. They may also recognize and create the necessary resources to reach their objectives.

9.2 Finding Leadership Opportunities

Individual Life

Finding chances for leadership in one's personal life is as crucial as finding them in the job. For instance, a leadership position in a volunteer group might provide one significant experience and transferable abilities for their professional life. Similarly, mentoring a younger member of your family or a friend may help you gain leadership experience.

Workplace

Finding leadership chances at work may include taking on more duties, volunteering for new initiatives, or assuming team leadership roles. For instance, a successful leader could offer to head the project team if a new initiative is being launched. By doing so, they assume responsibility for the initiative's success. Similarly, if a team is having trouble achieving its goals, a competent leader may provide direction and support to assist the team in succeeding.

Community

Participating in neighborhood groups or projects might help you find leadership possibilities in your community. Working with a non-profit group may provide a chance to hone leadership abilities while having a good social influence. Similarly, participating in neighborhood politics or community advocacy organizations may provide chances to take the lead and impact change.

Leaders are always looking for ways to have a good effect. People may see possibilities in their personal and professional lives and communities by cultivating the skills and attributes of good leaders. People may acquire important abilities and experiences that can help them succeed in all facets of their life by assuming leadership positions and responsibilities.

9.3 Taking on leadership roles

To effectively manage a team or organization, a leader needs various skills. With various chances and experiences, these qualities may be cultivated through time. The main topic of this chapter is the actions people may take to assume leadership responsibilities and develop into good leaders.

- Finding Leadership Opportunities: Finding leadership chances is one of the first stages in assuming a leadership position. These possibilities may be managing a little project or playing a bigger part in an organization. Retaining an open mind and looking for chances to hone your leadership abilities is crucial. Networking, requesting new responsibilities, and looking for mentoring or advice from seasoned leaders are all ways to do this.

- Building the Correct Mentality: Leadership positions require a certain mentality to accomplish goals while emancipating others. Successful leaders have a clear sense of direction and can inspire and encourage people to work together to achieve a shared objective. It's critical for people in leadership positions to have a positive, growth-oriented mentality that promotes learning, development, and resilience.

- Creating a Strong Team: Successful leaders know how crucial it is to have a strong team to succeed. They invest in fostering an environment that values responsibility, cooperation, and collaboration. Building connections with team members and fostering an atmosphere where everyone feels respected and supported are crucial when assuming leadership. This may be achieved by promoting open communication, highlighting unique skills, and offering professional growth opportunities.

- Establishing specific objectives and expectations is essential for success in leadership positions. Effective leaders who clearly communicate their vision create clear goals for their team or business. This promotes clarity of purpose, a feeling of responsibility, and accountability. The importance of realistic and reachable objectives cannot be overstated. Team members should be routinely updated on progress and given feedback.

- Leading by Example: Those in leadership positions must provide a positive example for their teams by acting per the morals and principles they espouse. This entails displaying a strong work ethic, accepting responsibility for errors, and behaving respectfully and empathetic toward others. Integrity and honesty are traits of effective leaders who are open and honest in their communications and decision-making.

- Continuous Learning and Improvement: A leadership position requires constant learning and development. Successful leaders invest in personal growth via education, training, and mentoring. They recognize the value of remaining current with industry trends and best practices. This enables them to remain abreast of developments and provide fresh viewpoints to their group or company.

Successful Leaders: Examples

Former PepsiCo CEO Indra Nooyi is renowned for her potent leadership abilities and dedication to creating a diverse and welcoming workplace. She stressed the value of listening to staff members, fostering open communication, and establishing clear expectations for her team.

Microsoft CEO Satya Nadella is renowned for fostering organizational creativity and leading with empathy. He has underlined the value of accepting change and allowing staff members to seize new possibilities.

Sheryl Sandberg is the COO of Facebook and an advocate for inclusion and diversity in the workplace. She is renowned for putting great emphasis on developing close bonds with team members and developing a climate of trust and cooperation.

Serving in a leadership capacity may be both difficult and rewarding. It necessitates developing various characteristics and talents, such as a growth-oriented mentality, effective communication skills, and an emphasis on team building. A person may develop into an effective leader and influence their businesses and communities by recognizing possibilities, establishing clear objectives, setting a good example, and engaging in ongoing learning and growth.

9.5 Continuing to develop leadership skills

Employers and educational institutions strongly appreciate leadership qualities in today's fast-paced and competitive environment. Having leadership qualities helps people improve personally and professionally, as well as in their future jobs. This book will examine several characteristics and talents of good leaders and ways to acquire such abilities in school and the future.

- Finding Leadership Opportunities: Leadership opportunities are the first step in building leadership abilities. College campuses have many leadership opportunities, including clubs, committees, and student groups. Outside of college, students might look for leadership positions via volunteer work, internships, and part-time employment. Students benefit from these chances by gaining important leadership and decision-making experience.
- Building Leadership Skills: By practice and experience, one may acquire effective leadership abilities. Communication, collaboration, problem-solving, decision-making, and time management are just a few of the crucial abilities to cultivate. Together with

emotional intelligence, flexibility, and the capacity to motivate and inspire people, effective leaders should also have these qualities.

- Communication: Effective leaders must have clear communication as a key competency. Leaders need to be able to articulate their ideas to their team members and actively listen to their worries. Giving and receiving feedback is a part of effective communication and helps to improve performance.
- Work as a team: Being a leader also entails working with others on a team. Collaboration and responsibility delegation should be skills of good leaders. They must be able to identify the advantages and disadvantages of each team member and delegate responsibilities appropriately.
- Effective problem-solving and decision-making abilities are crucial for leaders since they must deal with various obstacles. Leaders should be able to examine issues, weigh options, and reach

judgments using reason. Also, they must be able to adjust to shifting conditions and act quickly when required.

- Excellent time management abilities are a need for effective leaders. They should be able to assign duties, manage deadlines, and prioritize work. Maintaining a work-life balance is an important aspect of time management since it promotes personal performance and well-being.

- Emotional intelligence is the capacity to comprehend and control one's emotions and those of others. Successful leaders must be able to control their emotions and cope with stress. In addition, they must be able to foster a supportive workplace atmosphere and sympathize with others.

- Adaptability: Leaders must be able to change with the times and stay open-minded. Effective leaders should be receptive to fresh viewpoints and ideas to make better judgments.

- Inspiration and Motivation: Team members should be inspired and motivated by their leaders to accomplish their objectives. Effective leaders should develop a clear vision for the team and share it with everyone. They should also be able to encourage and reward team members since this raises spirits and motivation.

Gaining leadership abilities is crucial for both professional and personal advancement. Effective leadership skills may be built via practice and experience. To be a successful leader in college and in your future career, you must recognize leadership opportunities, develop critical skills like communication, teamwork, problem-solving, decision-making, and time management, and have emotional intelligence, adaptability, and the capacity to motivate and inspire others.

9.6 Lifelong learning and personal development

To remain relevant and successful in today's fast-evolving and fiercely competitive world, leaders must constantly advance themselves. For leaders to keep their skills, knowledge, and talents up to date, they must engage in personal growth and lifelong learning. This book will examine the value of personal growth and lifelong learning for successful leadership.

Why is continuing education crucial for leaders?

Adapting to the changing world: New technologies and concepts are developing at an unprecedented rate as the world changes more quickly. Leaders dedicated to lifelong learning may keep current on new developments and change.

Maintaining competition: In today's fiercely competitive corporate world, leaders are more likely to succeed if they are always working to improve. Leaders can stay ahead of the competition and remain relevant by maintaining their skills and expertise.

Personal and professional development: Leaders have the chance to grow personally and professionally due to lifelong learning. Leaders may enhance their performance, boost work satisfaction, and reach their professional objectives by learning new things.

Creating an attitude of lifelong learning:

- ❖ Curiosity: Those in leadership positions are more likely to be lifelong learners with an inquisitive mentality. They always consider fresh concepts, delve into new subjects, and search for novel encounters.
- ❖ Self-discipline and self-motivation are essential components of lifelong learning. Leaders dedicated to their growth are self-driven and prepared to invest the time and energy necessary to learn and advance.
- ❖ Humility: Those in leadership positions are more likely to learn effectively if they

are humble, open to new ideas, and prepared to own their ignorance. Humble leaders are more open to receiving criticism and new ideas, which is crucial for personal development.

❖ Resilience and tenacity are essential components of lifelong learning. Leaders who are prepared to keep going despite obstacles and failures are more likely to succeed personally and professionally.

Examples of leadership lifetime learning:

Elon Musk: Elon Musk is well-known for his dedication to lifelong learning. He is the CEO of Tesla and SpaceX. He has acknowledged that he reads for many hours daily and is always looking for fresh insights.

Warren Buffett is another example of a leader dedicated to lifelong learning. He is the CEO of Berkshire Hathaway. He is renowned for his love of reading and dedication to self-improvement.

Oprah Winfrey: The media magnate and philanthropist Oprah Winfrey is a lifelong learner who always seeks fresh perspectives. She has acknowledged that she reads several books each week and is always seeking methods to further her knowledge and skills.

In conclusion, successful leadership requires ongoing learning and personal growth. Leaders dedicated to lifelong learning can better meet the difficulties of a world that are changing quickly, maintain their level of expertise, and accomplish their personal and professional objectives. Leaders may improve their effectiveness, performance, and sense of fulfillment in their positions by adopting a lifelong learning mentality and actively searching out chances for personal improvement.

9.7 Building on past leadership experiences

Learning and experience may help you develop crucial leadership skills. Successful leaders draw on prior failures and successes to improve their leadership abilities. In this book, we will examine the value of building on prior leadership experiences and how it might result in improved leadership traits.

Reflecting on Previous Leadership Experiences: Reflecting on prior leadership experiences is crucial to develop into a successful leader. Leaders who reflect on their experiences may become better future leaders by learning from past failures and accomplishments. Leaders may recognize their strengths and limitations and take action to improve them by reflecting on prior experiences.

Learning from Mistakes: Leaders often make mistakes, but good leaders reflect on their errors and take preventative action. Leaders may learn from previous errors and prevent them from reoccurring by analyzing what went wrong and taking appropriate action. For instance, a manager who mismanaged task delegation would think back on the incident and strive to do better in the future.

Building on Successes: Skilful leaders need to study their failures and victories. Leaders may learn what worked effectively from prior successful leadership experiences and use similar tactics in future leadership positions by studying those experiences. For example, a leader who successfully guides a team through a challenging project might learn from the experience and use the tactics that work effectively in subsequent leadership responsibilities.

Applying previous leadership experiences to future roles:

Future leadership responsibilities may be built based on earlier leadership experiences. Successful leaders put the knowledge they have gained from prior experiences to use in their current leadership positions. They may improve their leadership abilities and become better leaders by doing this.

Elon Musk, the CEO of Tesla and SpaceX, is an example of a leader who has improved his prior leadership abilities. Musk has built a solid leadership foundation in his present responsibilities because of the several profitable businesses he has started in the past, including PayPal. Musk has used tactics that were successful in his former enterprises in his present leadership responsibilities, having learned from his past mistakes. For instance, Musk is recognized for focusing on innovation in his leadership at Tesla, a tactic successful at his previous firm, SpaceX.

In conclusion, effective leaders must build on their prior leadership experiences. It is possible to improve leadership abilities and produce better results by reflecting on previous experiences, learning from failures and achievements, and applying those lessons to future leadership situations. Leaders that are dedicated to both personal and professional development are individuals who build on their prior leadership experiences.

Conclusion

Throughout this book, we have looked at the characteristics and attributes of good leaders. We have addressed various issues, including group dynamics, ethical decision-making, establishing trust and respect, locating leadership possibilities, and personal growth. Below is a summary of the main ideas discussed in each chapter:

All leaders strive to encourage and inspire others to accomplish a common objective. Leaders come in many sizes, shapes, and personality types.

Empowering Strategies: Successful leaders encourage their teams to be creative and innovative, assign tasks and responsibilities, and provide feedback and support.

Creating a Mission Statement: For successful leadership, creating a clear and concise mission statement is crucial. It should embody the organization's underlying principles and goals and serve as a framework for decision-making. Successful leaders lead with a purpose by establishing clear objectives, using effective communication, and inspiring and motivating their teams to achieve those objectives.

Effective leadership requires a thorough understanding of group dynamics, including communication methods, dispute-resolution techniques, and decision-making procedures. *Developing Respect and Trust:* Effective leadership requires strong respect and trust. Leaders may earn people's respect and trust by being open, truthful, and dependable.

Conflict is unavoidable in every group or organization. Still, good leaders can foresee and deal with it by comprehending the underlying factors and putting the right conflict-resolution techniques in place. Successful leaders may settle disputes by carefully listening to all sides, being impartial, and cooperating to find a solution that benefits all parties.

Understanding Diversity: Diverse origins, experiences, and viewpoints are all celebrated by effective leaders who use these distinctions to spur innovation and development. Successful leaders promote inclusiveness by fostering an inclusive culture, appreciating each person, and ensuring everyone has an equal chance of success.

Successful leaders utilize ethical decision-making models to direct their decision-making processes, ensuring that they are fair, just, and consistent with the business's values. Values are crucial for successful leadership because they direct decision-making, influence company culture, and motivate followers.

Successful leaders are aware of their social responsibilities, including their effects on society, the environment, and their stakeholders, and they strive to bring about constructive change. Successful leaders demonstrate empathy by actively listening to and comprehending the needs and views of their followers. They then utilize this knowledge to make choices that are in the best interests of society as a whole.

Personal Responsibility: Successful leaders accept full accountability for their decisions, owning up to their errors and acting to correct them. Successful leaders make sure that they and their followers are accountable for their choices and actions. Successful leaders recognize and grab all leadership chances, including ones that may arise unexpectedly.

Assuming Leadership Positions: Successful leaders assume leadership positions by exhibiting self-assurance, initiative, and a desire to grow. Successful leaders cultivate their leadership abilities via continuous study, introspection, and practice, positioning themselves for academic achievement and future employment. Successful leaders are dedicated to lifelong learning and personal growth, always looking for ways to better their businesses and themselves.

After looking at numerous characteristics and attributes of good leaders, readers should consider and use the following essential takeaways in their own lives:

Exceptional leaders are motivated by a distinct and compelling mission that urges others to support their cause. Leaders need emotional intelligence and empathy to better create collaboration, respect, and trust among their team members.

Relationship development and maintenance are essential: Leaders who emphasize developing connections with their team members and stakeholders are likely to accomplish their objectives and develop a devoted following. Leaders that place a higher value on moral judgment than temporary benefits acquire followers' respect and trust and are more likely to persuade others to follow their example.

Responsibility and accountability are crucial: Exceptional leaders are prepared to accept responsibility for their choices and actions and take ownership of the results.

Personal growth and lifelong learning are essential: Successful leaders continue to learn and grow personally to increase their talents, skills, and knowledge.

The main lesson from this book is that leadership is a collection of abilities, traits, and behaviors that anybody can acquire and hone. Readers may become more successful leaders in their own lives and have a good influence on the world by using the principles and examples from this book.

Successful leadership involves not just having particular characteristics and abilities but also constantly developing one's leadership abilities and having a good influence on society. This chapter's call to action encourages readers to keep honing their leadership skills and using them to improve the world. Leadership is a dynamic attribute that can be developed and refined through time rather than being a static one. As a result, it's important to keep improving one's leadership abilities over time. Continuous learning, mentoring relationships, and exposure to novel situations help with this.

For the development of leadership qualities, lifelong learning is essential. Finding classes, seminars, and other learning opportunities that emphasize leadership development is one method to do this. These courses may give participants a greater comprehension of leadership ideas and useful tools for enhancing their leadership skills. Another important component of developing leadership is mentoring. Mentors may provide advice, encouragement, and criticism to assist people in improving their leadership abilities. Mentors may be found in various contexts, including the workplace, community groups, and educational institutions.

The development of leadership abilities also depends on exposure to new situations. This might include assuming new tasks and obligations, such as managing a team or donating your time to become a leader in a neighborhood group. People may learn useful skills from these experiences, including good communication, conflict resolution, and decision-making.

Successful leaders use their talents to change the world for the better. This may be accomplished in several ways, including engaging in volunteer work, being an active member of society, or managing organizations with a beneficial influence. An effective approach for people to change the world is via community service. People may hone their leadership abilities while improving their communities by volunteering for neighborhood groups or participating in service initiatives.

Another approach for people to utilize their leadership abilities to create change is via social action. This may include leading social movements that try to alleviate social injustice and inequality or campaigning for issues reflecting one's ideals. Another method for people to utilize their leadership abilities to make a difference is to lead organizations that do so. This may include founding one's own company, managing a nonprofit, or managing an enterprise with a conscience.

The characteristics and attributes of good leaders, as well as many subjects connected to leadership development, have all been covered in this book. It has given readers useful tips and tools for enhancing their leadership abilities and positively affecting the world. Each reader must take these revelations and put them into practice by honing their leadership skills and using them to improve their communities and the globe. Everyone may become a successful leader and significantly influence the world if they put their mind to it, work hard, and commit to lifelong learning.